LA VIE EN ROSE

25

π   59419

XX

LA VIE EN ROSE

LIVING IN FRANCE

SUZANNE LOWRY

PHOTOGRAPHS BY **TIM CLINCH**

BULFINCH PRESS

AOL TIME WARNER BOOK GROUP

BOSTON NEW YORK LONDON

Text copyright © 2003 by Suzanne Lowry
Photographs copyright © 2003 by Tim Clinch
Compilation copyright © 2003 by Pavilion Books Limited

All rights reserved. No part of this book may be reproduced in any form or by any electronic or mechanical means, including information storage and retrieval systems, without permission in writing from the publisher, except by a reviewer who may quote brief passages in a review.

First United States Edition

First published in Great Britain in 2003 by Pavilion Books Limited

Designed by Nigel Partridge

ISBN 0-8212-2808-0
Library of Congress Control Number 2002116458

Bulfinch Press is a division of AOL Time Warner Book Group.

Printed in Singapore

Front cover: Christopher Hope and Ingrid Hudson's house, La Maison Verte, Minervois
Back cover: The home of Jacques de Crussol, Le Duché d'Uzès, Provence

CONTENTS

INTRODUCTION 6

CHAPTER ONE

THE GRAND STYLE

Memoires de la Gloire

Jacques de Crussol – Le Duché d'Uzès,
Provence 12

Philippine de Ganay – Château de Courances,
Ile de France 20

Patricia and Philip Hawkes – Château de
Missery, Burgundy 28

Bob and Isabelle Higgins – Château de Mail,
Gascony 38

Luc and Beatrice Viennet – Seigneurie de Peyrat,
Languedoc 48

Geneviève Leroy – Château de Fajac,
Lauragais 56

CHAPTER TWO

PARIS CHIC

La Vie de Bohème

Charlotte Mosley – Apartment in
Faubourg-Saint-Germain 66

Valerio Adami – Apartment in Montmartre 74

Victor Koulbak – Studio in Montparnasse 82

Djamila Taulé – Loft in Belleville 90

Dimonah and Mehmet Iksel – Apartment
in Le Sentier 100

Agnès Comar – Apartment
on the Rive Gauche 108

VISITOR'S GUIDE 190

INDEX 191

ACKNOWLEDGEMENTS 192

CHAPTER THREE

LIFE IN THE COUNTRY

Le Bonheur est dans le Pré

Jacques Grange – Mas Mireio, Provence 120

Pierre Passebon – La Ferme Blanche,
Touraine 130

Christopher Hope and Ingrid Hudson –
La Maison Verte, Minervois 138

Ken Hom – La Tour Hugues de Sabanac,
La Vallée du Lot 146

Lesleigh – Le Jardin Secret,
Luberon 154

Michel and Christine Guérard – Les Prés
de Eugénie, Landes 164

Gilles Sacksick – La Roche, Quercy 172

Christain Liaigre – Ancien Monastère,
Ile de Ré 180

INTRODUCTION

A dream of life in France, whether in a moated chateau, a simple stone farmhouse or a Parisian aerie, is shared by people of almost every nation. Many turn the dream into reality, coming to this vast, underpopulated country with its diverse climates, stunning landscapes and civilized quality of life apparently impervious to the worst erosion of modern development, to embrace *la vie Française*.

This is nothing new. From earliest times, invasion and population shifts have brought influences from elsewhere to marry with a natural Gallic flair, making France an eternal melting pot for architectural styles and decorative fashion. Cultural influences spread from the south and east across the Mediterranean, while Nordic and Germanic trends came from the cold north. It is impossible to travel through the modern country without being impressed by the extraordinary variety of traditions that have been absorbed and adapted. Prehistoric caves, medieval castles, great palaces, simple stone dwellings and half-timbered farmhouses, bourgeois apartments, Bohemian garrets and futuristic villas all go to make France a living museum of domestic habitat.

The Roman remains in the south are glimpses of classical antiquity, not just the great amphitheatres and arches but the mosaic floors of graceful villas or precious jewellery and domestic ornaments fished from the sea and dug up from vineyards. In a single medieval village, architectural layers can show how the defensive, military construction of the long age of war and chaos gave way to that of commercial prosperity and the hope of living a good life in peace. By the golden age of building in the seventeenth and eighteenth centuries, castles were no longer moated and fortified, but opened outwards to elegantly sculptured landscapes. The world was seen not through an arrow-slit in a bleak tower, but from lofty windows looking onto luscious gardens of water and green mazes, towards forests made for hunting, not fighting. Courances, home of the de Ganay family near Paris, is one of the most beautiful examples: here if anywhere *La Vie en Rose* – a sweet, idyllic life, in the usual English interpretation – must have seemed possible for the ruling few, walking between well-trimmed hedges while the happy *paysans* frolicked as they made hay, like characters from a *toile de Jouy* fabric.

By 1789 the *noblesse* may have been walking on "rose petals strewn over the abyss" but, in spite of the Revolution, its great castles – more than 40,000 of them – still dot the landscape. Many are in ruins or states of severe neglect, but in recent years efforts to preserve and restore grand old houses have markedly increased. In the southern city of Uzès the young Duke is reviving, after

Above: The bell tower and galleried façade of the restored Couvent aux Herbes, an old school building in which Christine Guérard has created a haven of peace and beauty for guests at Eugénie les Bains.

Left: American Isabelle Higgins decorated the lofty drawing room of the Château de Mail in Gascony with nuanced colours that pick up the morning light.

Opposite: Chef Ken Hom's superb kitchen in his home at Catus in the Lot Valley. On his Maestro range he cooks the best of the rich produce of the region. Guests can watch as ducks are roasted on the spit in the chimney. The well-chosen still life above it is by P Van Deer.

Above: The stone steps that lead to artist Gilles Sacksick's house in the Quercy region. In this gentle, idyllically French setting, he paints what he sees around him.

generations of neglect, dispossession and profligacy, the magnificent *Duché*, his ancestral home, part palace, part fortress. Patricia and Philip Hawkes, passionate English devotees of the *vieilles pierres* (ancient buildings) of France, live surrounded by the moat of the fairytale Château de Missery in Burgundy. Nearly a thousand kilometres away to the southwest, in the Landes, Michel and Christine Guérard have created a little universe of excellence in health, cuisine and décor at Les Prés d'Eugénie.

Everywhere modest and disused agricultural buildings have been transformed into bucolic dream-houses by restoration that is, above all, "authentic", although at times authenticity may have a patina of fantasy. Parisian decorator Jacques Grange has created a perfect rustic haven in Van Gogh's Provence; artist Gilles Sacksick's small stone house in Quercy is recorded and reinvented in his paintings; Ingrid Hudson has conceived a neo-retro style for her tiny medieval house in the Languedoc. In these homes, as in myriad *mazets* (small stone cottages) and *chaumières* (thatched cottages) from Provence to Normandy, it is not a question of restoration in any academic sense, more of personal re-invention.

La Vie en Rose opens doors on an assortment of people who have imposed their ideas on traditional French forms, or have created original atmospheres in houses, apartments and chateaux. In his photographs Tim Clinch makes a superb and seductive use of natural light, showing the results not just as houses but catching some of the imaginative *esprit* of the owners. For this is not a book about decoration and design only, but aims to show how individuals express their personalities in the homes they make.

French adherence to calculated perfection and a fixed stylistic canon has, in recent years, been nibbled away at the edges by influential decorators – such as the minimalist Andrée Putman and the eclectic, post-modernist Philippe Starck – and by the editors of magazines such as *Marie Claire Maison* and *Côté Sud* propagating a looser, more expressive style of living. Distressed wood and peeling walls in original natural colours have been accepted, and authenticity and insouciance have replaced studious classicism. At the same time, the French, long neglectful of their rural heritage except where food was concerned, are now being inspired to repossess their crumbling *manoirs* and farms and to back the revival of old techniques and materials to restore country furniture and artifacts. At government level an active Ministry of Culture declares its commitment to the preservation and rescue of the *patrimoine*, but the task would be hopeless were it not for the devotion of private citizens to the refurbishment – and maintenance – of glorious houses and gardens.

France, at the centre of Europe, is still a magnet for artists, thinkers and designers. No one can live there and be impervious to French attitudes and flair; at the same time foreign input constantly enlivens a culture that can too easily become rigid and smug. This is why half the houses in this collection are foreign-owned.

Foreigners may take a rosier view of life in their adopted – or borrowed – country than the French, who read implications of delusion and folly into the words of Edith Piaf's famous song. But although falling in love with French houses and lifestyle may sometimes be foolish, it is also incorrigible. "Everyone has two homelands, their own and *La France*," Thomas Jefferson famously quipped. Two centuries later this is truer than ever.

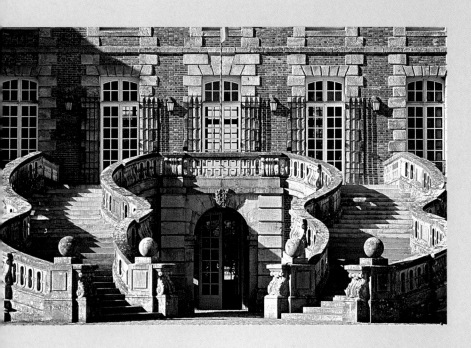

THE GRAND STYLE

Memoires de la Gloire

France is a republic that proudly recalls its magnificent royal and aristocratic past, witnessed by more than 40,000 chateaux scattered around the country. Austere medieval keeps mark the scenes of distant wars while moated Renaissance piles of the Loire Valley and superb palaces around Paris recall the glories of François I and the Sun King, Louis XIV. Some castles are windswept ruins, others state property or public museums. But many are in private hands, the owners striving to preserve precious buildings and craftsmanship while adapting and reinventing the grand style for the modern world.

LE DUCHE D'UZES

JACQUES DE CRUSSOL: PROVENCE

Right: A view from one of the Duché's towers, showing the old castle walls and the town tight up against them.

Left: The ducal family's private courtyard-garden was redesigned by Jacques de Crussol and features lavender borders and large half-glazed terra-cotta pots.

Above: Jacques and Alessandra de Crussol with their son, Charles.

Jacques de Crussol, seventeenth Duc d'Uzès, is an elegant and meticulous man. As he crunches across his well-ordered and densely gravelled inner courtyard-garden, explaining the ups and downs of his ancient family and the complex jigsaw of architectural styles that comprise his ancestral home, he swoops to pounce on a lone dead chestnut leaf, crackling it in his hand like a scrap of dry parchment. No detail escapes him in his mission to restore his Duché, a precious piece of France's heritage, to its former glory.

Uzès, a jewel of a town founded 2,000 years ago by the Romans as a castrum for their regional capital of Nîmes, is set in a place of vigilance between the Pont du Gard, the magnificent aqueduct, the Cévennes, which rise in wooded softness to the northwest, and the Rhône to the east. The existing buildings span the centuries from feudal times through the Renaissance to the eighteenth century and recent restoration projects have made Uzès – vying with it's illustrious neighbours Avignon and Arles – increasingly attractive to tourists. The Place aux Herbes, with its golden stone arcades and imposing townhouses, has become a symbol of old meridional France – the Midi. Many films, including *Cyrano de Bergerac*, have used it as a location.

The Duché, a fortress-cum-palace with a line of disparate towers dominating the skyline like the remains of some medieval Manhattan, for a time rather lagged behind the rest of the town in restoration. However, the arrival of the current incumbent has brought fresh dynamism (and financial investment) to the task.

"It is a twenty-year project," says the duke. "We are about halfway through. For the first ten years it has been ninety percent structure and ten percent decoration. For the next decade it will be ninety percent décor and ten percent structure, which will be more fun."

This part of France has had a turbulent history since the Romans left, surviving barbarian invasions (fifth century), the crusade against the Cathars (thirteenth century), Wars of Religion (sixteenth century), and then the Revolution of 1789 when the Duché narrowly escaped total demolition after the duke of the time fled to exile in England.

Left: The Grand Salon in the Renaissance wing is filled with family portraits and Louis XV furniture. An unusual feature of this enormous, elegant room is its four magnificent white marble fireplaces, one in each corner. The originals were removed at the time of the Revolution, but the present duke has had replacements specially made in Carrara marble – although some inspired guesswork had to go into the designs. The elaborate stucco-work on the blue walls has also been restored and replaced where necessary.

Right: A corner of the salon, whose high windows overlook the main courtyard. The superb façade has the family arms and motto, Ferro non auro *(by the sword and not by gold) carved in stone above the main doorway, showing an honorable preference for armed combat over riches.*

A property speculator bought the palace intending to sell it off piecemeal. He ripped out many fireplaces and stripped rooms of furniture and artefacts. He then found that this wasn't a profit-making operation and sold the palace to a consortium of Uzès families who rented it out. The tenth duke managed to reacquire it after the restoration of the monarchy and undertook some rebuilding, as did his successors. However, as the present duke remarks dryly, his forbears had a bad habit of running out of money – "Four generations of my family ruined themselves" – something he is determined not to do, managing his own affairs with considerable business acumen.

If the duke's ancestors were a touch profligate, the women of the family were charismatic, and it was the money and inspiration of the fifteenth duchess that came to the rescue of the family home. "She was a very remarkable woman – she not only saved the Duché, but the town itself," her grandson says. Known as "la Marquise Rouge", she was notoriously the *éminence grise* behind

Left: The yellow bedroom, also known as the Ambassador's room, includes a bust made by "the Grand Duchess" Anne in the corner. The bed is dressed in classic Louis XVI style, and the floor retains the original tomettes, *highly polished red hexagonal tiles.*

Right: Hunting trophies dominate the dining hall in the Renaissance wing and a tryptych of family portraits hangs at the far end. The ceiling is a fine example of plafond à la française – *a series of narrow beams held up by heavy crossbeams.*

Daladier, the prewar prime minister of France. Later she became good friends with André Malraux, de Gaulle's minister of culture, who passed the first law aimed at saving France's historic sites. The indomitable duchess made sure that Uzès went to the top of the list for salvation, although she never managed to lure the urbane politician to see her remote provincial fief.

Jacques de Crussol inherited part of his grandmother's fortune and a determination to bring her work to fruition. Even before he came into the ducal title in 2001, at the age of forty-four, he had taken over the property and begun work. His main home is in Paris, but he carved out a minute apartment for himself in one corner of the ancestral agglomeration. He and his Italian wife, Alessandra, and young son, Charles, still use this *garçonnière* while awaiting completion of the large and airy private apartments overlooking the Cour d'Honneur. The miniature vaulted dining room and kitchen, cosy bedroom and bathroom are in dramatic contrast to the vast halls and rooms of the rest of the palace.

Wide stone stairs lead from the apartment to another world. Grand rooms open off a long corridor hung with a line of modern Venetian glass chandeliers, a light touch added by the duke. The dining room, where soon after our visit he was preparing to receive forty guests representing the *noblesse* of Languedoc, is hung with family portraits and antlers, plus a large Aubusson tapestry depicting a mythical battle.

Since so many of the Duché's treasures have been sold off or lost, Jacques de Crussol has to search for appropriate replacements. In particular he seeks family portraits. The best pictures he sends to Paris for restoration, but much of the work is done in an *atelier* set up in an unoccupied wing where pictures and furniture are also stored, as if in a grand props room or an opera house.

Above: A striking marble bust of Anne, Duchess d'Uzès, on a marble mantelpiece in the library, where many family books and memoirs are kept.

16

Right: A window looks out onto cypress trees, with the red tiles of the town roofs visible beyond.

Below: The present duke takes his role as the guardian of family history and tradition seriously. Here are some of the specially bound annual archives, which are safely stored in the library.

Left: The library is the repository of historic books and Crussol family archives. Ceremonial state costumes and military uniforms are also on show here. The French cavalry helmet with its long, horsehair tail was once worn by a nineteenth-century duke.

In one of the bedrooms hangs a portrait of "La Grande Duchesse", formerly Anne de Rochechouart, heiress to the Veuve Cliquot champagne fortune and a dashing personality of nineteenth-century society. A sculptor and a poet, she also campaigned for women's rights and was the first woman to get a driving licence in France and to fly in an airplane.

Everywhere in the grand rooms are reminders of the Crussol family's past glory. "I am premier duke and first peer of France," explains Jacques de Crussol with a wistful smile. "The equivalent of the Duke of Norfolk in England. In the past the Dukes of Uzès carried the crown and sceptre at the coronation and had the right to pronounce the accession of the king – '*Le roi est mort! Vive le roi!* '

Ceremonial costumes and velvet cloaks, plumed hats and swords bear silent witness to this in a glass case in the library.

Jacques de Crussol is the seventeenth duke, and the title goes back through twenty-five generations, so it is not surprising that he is driven by a sense of history. The whole history of France is contained in the family archives and the duke believes that the long tradition still has value in the modern world. As duke, he feels a duty to preserve a certain standard, a certain elegance of life. Some of the palace rooms are available for rent so others can share his heritage and experience something of his life while contributing to the upkeep of the enormous building.

France is a secular Republic but, locally at least, old loyalties die hard. Monsieur le Duc may no longer have his own army, but he has an enthusiastic team of helpers who run eagerly to his call. Opening the gates of the palace to tourists is not just a question of making money: the duke believes it is all part of his latter-day seigneurial duty and helps to forge important links with the town.

CHATEAU DE COURANCES

Right: The austere seventeenth-century façade of the Château de Courances was later embellished by a magnificent stone staircase of honour, a smaller copy of one at nearby Fontainebleau.

Left: A view from the salon showing the tranquil formal lake that mirrors the building. The chateau is built on a site with twelve springs, and the gardens were created by André Le Nôtre.

Below: The grand canal is well shaded by the trees that make a walk in the park at Château de Courances such a great pleasure.

The Ile de France, the circle of fertile, now heavily populated, territory around Paris, has been the central seat of power since the Dark Ages, and eventually lent its name to the whole country.

It was the royal fief and in the seventeenth century, when it was (*hubris*, perhaps) deemed safe to live in civilized peace in unfortified domains, it became more than a protective hinterland and playground. Louis XIV made the great chateau at Versailles, to the west of Paris, not only his hunting lodge but the seat of the most elegant and dazzling court in Europe. His nobles and vassals were required to be in attendance (unless banished) and deserted their estates in *la France profonde* to build or rebuild castles and mansions in the region, the better to revolve around the Sun King. The result was a catalogue of the most beautiful classical and baroque houses, whose names resonate through history: Chantilly, Fontainebleau, Rambouillet, Compiègne, Vaux-le-Vicomte.

Miraculously, most have survived wars and revolutions to delight visitors today and some are still family homes. Courances is perhaps the most enchanting of these, a relatively unembellished seventeenth-century house (with some later additions) whose fame and greatest charm lies in the water from the twelve springs on the site. The house is surrounded by a monumental system of canals and water gardens, offset by intricate box-hedge *parterres* laid out by the great landscape designer André Le Nôtre. Stretches of glassy, ornamental water mirror the house and statuary on all sides; stone dolphins belch cascades into the stillness and the sound of rushing water is constant.

"Even after all these years", says the present marquise, Philippine de Ganay, who has lived at Courances since her marriage more than half a century ago, "I still wake up and think – Is it raining? Ah, no, of course it is just the waterfalls ."

In common with the best architecture of the period, Courances mixes grandeur with a kind of intimacy and sweetness. It was manifestly a place dedicated to the enjoyment of all the good things of life, although history has not always permitted this.

The estate, close to Milly-la-Fôret, fifty kilometres south of Paris, dates from the thirteenth century. The present house was built to replace a medieval castle and has been in the Ganay

Left: Beech trees shed leaves on the immaculately kept lawns, tended these days by only two gardeners under the supervision of the Marquise de Ganay herself.

Right: The vaulted arcade under the main terrace provides a pleasantly cool area in which to sit and relax in the summer.

Below: A disused mill in the Japanese garden is one of the surprises at Courances. Created nearly a century ago by the mother of the present marquis, its exotic trees and shrubs offer a riot of leaf colour around a water-lily pool fed by this waterfall.

family for just over a century, before which it belonged to a sequence of ambitious courtiers and churchmen. The present marquis and marquise have divided the house up into four large apartments, one for themselves and one each for their three daughters and their young families.

Daughter of the Duc and Duchesse de Mouchy, Philippine de Ganay grew up not far away at Fontainebleau, where her mother owned the Ermitage de Pompadour. She was thus a neighbour and often visited Courances to play with the five de Ganay boys. She married Jean-Louis, heir to the title, just before the outbreak of the Second World War and saw Courances occupied by German forces. All the same, the damage at Courances was considerable. "They built what amounted to a small town in the gardens and when they left they blew up their munitions store," she recalls. After the Liberation, the house became an American hospital and then the residence of Field-Marshal Montgomery, while he was at Fontainbleau as Deputy Supreme Commander of Nato. "He asked my father-in-law if he could live here for a short while," says Madame de Ganay. "And then stayed for seven years! He was a very austere man. His only pleasure appeared to be a game of billiards with his batman in the evenings." Monty's billiard table is still in the games room and his flagstaff can be found in front of the house, although now the Ganay family arms fly from it. "We only put our flag up because the pole was there," says Madame la Marquise with a shrug.

Her husband, Jean-Louis, was a Resistance hero during the war, narrowly escaping with his life. On his return home they set about helping to repair the damage and devastation, a task that took many years to complete.

"I added a lot of cushions and comfort to the private rooms," Madame de Ganay says. "It was all a bit severe and uncomfortable." But above all she was, and still is, concerned with the gardens, which were in a state of near ruin. The stunning Japanese garden, created in the 1920s by her late mother-in-law, Berthe, Marquise de Ganay, was full of mud and almost beyond rescue; today it is one of the wonders of Courances – a colourful and exotic counterpoint to the rest of the park.

Berthe was the granddaughter of Baron Heber, the man who bought and restored Courances in the 1870s, when it was also in a terrible state of dilapidation. (It was described by artist Jules Le Coeur, after a visit in 1866 with Renoir and Sisley, as "decomposing slowly like a lump of sugar forgotten in a damp place".) Berthe married Hubert de Ganay and they continued to resuscitate

Above: The impressive grand salon at the main entrance is furnished in seventeenth-century style. A bas-relief portrait of Louis XIV, the Sun King, surmounts a magnificent red marble fireplace.

Below: The chateau's game room features a carved Renaissance fireplace. The trophies on top were brought back from African safaris by the Marquis de Ganay.

Below right: A brick-vaulted corridor leads to the game room. More antlers and a varied display of straw hats provides something of an English country house atmosphere.

this phoenix-like property. An exquisite portrait of Berthe, appropriately by the Japanese artist Fujita, is on public display in the house.

Philippine de Ganay comes from a family of gardeners: her mother created a famous *potager* (ornamental vegetable garden) and her uncle, the Vicomte de Noailles, was president of the Royal Horticultural Society in England. One of her best friends was the late Rosemary Verey, and to this day Madame de Ganay frequently accompanies groups of French gardening enthusiasts to England, a great source of inspiration. At Courances she whizzes about the *allées* on her mini tractor. "It is a wonderful machine," she says proudly. "I don't ever let anyone else use it, because I am so reliant on it. I cannot possibly walk the distances now." When it is not in use she parks it unceremoniously but conveniently at the door to the private apartments, underneath the *escalier d'honneur*, which was added to the house in the nineteenth century and is a scaled-down copy of one at Fontainebleau.

They open the park and part of the chateau to the public at weekends and 25,000 people visit every year. This sounds impressive, but the numbers are falling; the marquise is resigned to the fact that people travel abroad these days and, as she puts it, don't want to see something that is on their doorstep. However, the income from visitors, plus an "inadequate" grant from the state, helps to keep the place going. But it is run without resident servants and only two gardeners – a shoestring operation.

Left: The study with ornately
embroidered seventeenth-
century chairs and richly
carved boiseries (oak
panelling). The billiard table
used by Field-Marshal
Montgomery when he lived
here is still ready for play.

At the chapel door is posted a polite reminder, in the Marquise's own handwriting, to visitors that they should remember to tip the guide. "The English never tip – everyone else does, even the Italians. It is not that they are mean; they are just not used to it."

Both de Ganays speak almost accent-free English, thanks to English nannies and (for the Marquis) his time in London during the war. They have given Courances some of the atmosphere of an English country house, especially in their private apartment, where are to be found hunting trophies from Africa, a corridor hung with antlers and straw hats, and the aforementioned comfortable cushions and armchairs.

The house is full of curiosities and treasures, well worth a small gratuity on top of the entrance charge, notably the rare sixteenth-century "monkey tapestries" that hang in the library. But the greatest pleasure of Courances is to walk in the gardens, watching the light change on the water, to see the giant perch in an underwater scramble under the kitchen windows and to have a glimpse of a world and a society long gone and yet, thanks to the efforts of its descendants, still with us.

Above and right: The main
dining room, which is in the
part of the chateau open to
the public, is still used by the
family. The high windows
with their silk blinds have a
superb view over the gardens.
A mixed collection of plates,
found when the chateau was
being restored, make a frieze
around the top of the room.
A pair of nineteenth-century
candelabra stand on a buffet.

CHATEAU DE MISSERY

PATRICIA AND PHILIP HAWKES: BURGUNDY

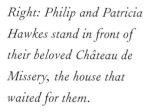

Right: Philip and Patricia Hawkes stand in front of their beloved Château de Missery, the house that waited for them.

Left: The façade of the chateau that had fallen into neglect and was bought by an American architect, who came to buy only a stone balustrade.

Right: A detail from an old stone wall, which leads up to the chateau.

The ancient Duchy of Burgundy is often regarded as the spiritual and political heart of France: a rich land producing incomparable wines and dotted with villages in golden stone, chateaux and churches.

Down the centuries Burgundy has been in the thick of power struggles and its rulers were often more powerful than the kings whom they helped to make and break. During the Hundred Years' War, Duke Philippe sided with the English and his forces took Joan of Arc prisoner; but soon after her death he changed sides and Joan's desire to clear *les Anglais* out of France was at last achieved. Centuries later, some of the earliest rumblings of the French Revolution were heard in Dijon, the Burgundian capital.

Abbeys and sacred places abound, notably the great Romanesque church of Vézelay, on which thousands of pilgrims converge every year. Saint Bernard preached the Second Crusade here and more peaceful monks began the tradition of viticulture, which still sustains the region, while many noble houses and castles recall the glorious past.

Château de Missery, in the aptly named Côte d'Or (Gold Coast) *département*, looks just as a picture-book chateau should, with medieval round towers and a moat offsetting the elegant eighteenth-century façade.

The current owners, Philip and Patricia Hawkes, sell chateaux to others and they have managed to acquire a gem as their own home. The site, Patricia explains, has been occupied since around the eighth century, when the earth was dug out to create a mound or *motte*. This probably had some kind of wooden structure on it, which later was replaced by stone and eventually by a fully-fledged fortified medieval castle. The two round towers and moat are what remains of a typical Burgundian *chateau fort*, which would have had four towers and a curtain wall. After the end of the Hundred Years' War security was relaxed somewhat and the protective wall was partly removed.

Above and left: The magnificent potager, *or formal flower and vegetable garden, is one of the delights of the chateau's expansive grounds and still provides the household with all the produce it requires.*

Then in the mid-eighteenth century a local parliamentarian from Dijon, Jean-Baptiste de Flamardin de Suremien, used his second wife's dowry to pull down most of what was left of the old castle and replaced it with the present building – a perfect classical house. No one has been able to find out who the architect was, but the work took ten years, and the proud owner then lived in his house peaceably through the upheavals of the Revolution and the Napoleonic period, before dying in 1818. (Patricia Hawkes believes that Missery is a house that looks after the people who live in it; nothing calamitous or dreadful has ever happened there.)

The Suremien family continued to own the house until, by 1922, there was only an Abbé and his two sisters left living in near-poverty with, it is said, chickens in the salon. Missery's luck turned that year, however, when a celebrated American architect named McLenaghan came to call. He was building a house in Tuxedo Park in the United States and needed a balustrade; some-one recommended Missery's, but when he saw it he decided that it would be a crime to

Right: The rear façade and the moat which sometimes freezes in winter, allowing the World Ice Croquet Championships to take place. These events are always won by Philip Hawkes.

30

*Left: The paved stone
floor and back staircase
area is where summer straw
hats and assorted bric-à-brac
find their place.*

*Right: The kitchen
has a monastic table for
simple meals, with vegetables
from the garden. Patricia
Hawkes's collection of
antique coat hangers is a
reminder of guests past.*

*Below: Tall windows look out
onto the courtyard.*

remove it. So he bought the whole house instead. McLenaghan died soon after that, but left the chateau, complete with balustrade, to his small grandson Mike, with the use of it to his parents. Mike spent much of his childhood here and used it until the Hawkses bought it from him in 1979, after a long courtship. Philip had seen the house a decade earlier and tried to rent it, but a cousin of the owner got in before him. Patricia believes that houses choose their owners and that Missery waited for them: "It gave us time to meet and marry and settle down a bit and get our business going."

The chance to buy came along just as they were on the point of renting Château d'Yvil in Normandy. "We always say that we have been delivered from Yvil and brought into Missery," says Patricia. The name however has no gloomy resonance it – is just a local place name: "We always say our Missery is our joy."

Left: A grand piano in the main entrance hall where many concerts are held, thanks to the excellent acoustics.

Below: A small antique side-table with several glass vases.

The couple have lived in the house rather as Patricia was used to as a child in her family's large house in Somerset. It is open house for all her friends, who sometimes become more involved in *la vie du château* than they bargained for, put to work in useful restoration.

The glory of the house is the entrance hall and its two *escaliers d'honneur*. The main staircase collapsed and (fortunately for them) was rebuilt just before the Hawkeses bought Missery. The superb cast-iron banister was in pieces and took months to reassemble and repair. The acoustics in the hall are so good that it is often used for concerts and musical evenings.

The salon, the central room of the house, is lined by especially beautiful *boiseries* (panelling), which were brought by Jean-Baptiste Suremien from a house in Dijon. It is probable that he intended to line the walls of all the main rooms, according to the style of the day, but did not complete the project.

34

Below: The salon contains a happy mix of French and English furniture. The original panelling was brought from a townhouse in Dijon in the eighteenth century. Guests gather here before dinner, always correctly dressed.

The Hawkses have their offices and a small apartment in Paris: Missery is for weekends (about one in five) and holidays. One of the attractions of Burgundy is its accessibility from the capital. They take the business of living in a chateau seriously and delight in telling people how it can be done in modern times, without the army of servants that such places once called for.

The long dining table is always laid absolutely correctly and weekend guests are asked to dress for dinner. Patricia Hawkes thinks it is nice for people who have been walking or working in the garden all day to change into "something that is fitting to the scene". It is good for young people, she reckons, to have a sense of moving upwards towards a more civilized life rather than downwards to the lowest common denominator all the time. While Patricia is putting finishing touches to the meal, Philip will be left to "*faire salon*" – pour drinks, make introductions and keep the conversation going. The salon is a formal French room but with touches of chintzy country-house comfort added, such as the sofa imported from England.

Less formal meals are eaten in the kitchen on a lovely long table brought from Somerset; diners are surveyed by a large stag's head over the chimney piece and by Patricia's growing collection of antique coat hangers. The menu will always include delicious vegetables from the large walled *potager*, which appears on plans of the property that predate the existing house. The garden also produces a wonderful range of flowers for cutting, and in the centre is a huge circular stone *bassin*, eleven metres across, which is sometimes used as a swimming pool.

Guests are expected to follow certain rules: keeping the doors shut, for instance, especially in winter, and the windows fastened, as a sudden gust can cause the loss of precious old window panes. The elements are the chateau's worst enemies, although if the moat freezes over skating is fun. Philip has instigated the World Ice Croquet Championships, which he always wins.

Philip and Patricia were fortunate that Missery was in good condition. By their own account they have done little more than clean it up, polish the floors and so on. Their aim has been to emulate the loving care given it by its American owners, and this will be continued by their daughter Lucy, who is already taking a proud and responsible interest in her heritage.

Above: The main staircase, which collapsed and was rebuilt to perfection. The light from the long windows catches the lines of the antique sledge.

Right: The main bedroom has a high-canopied bed – a typical French bateau-lit.

CHATEAU DE MAIL

BOB AND ISABELLE HIGGINS: GASCONY

Left: The east-facing main living room, for which Isabelle Higgins mixed a rosy-gold wall-colour that echoes the natural light that floods in. Her pink and ecru silk panelled curtains do likewise. The painting is by Anne Tabachnik.

Right: Bob and Isabelle Higgins dance on the terrace of the magnificent house they have saved from ruin.

Above: A glimpse of the house through ivy on an elegant Italianate arcade.

Right: The front door and part of the main façade of the Château de Mail, now beautifully restored.

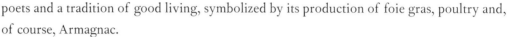

Gascony, a proud and ancient province, was the birthplace of D'Artagnan, the fiery and insolently flamboyant hero of *The Three Musketeers*, and something of his bold "musketeer spirit" is said to survive here. Stretching westwards from Toulouse to the Atlantic, it has been, even by French standards, a territory ravaged by war and invasion; but it has also bred troubadour poets and a tradition of good living, symbolized by its production of foie gras, poultry and, of course, Armagnac.

At the eastern end lies the *département* of the Gers, as green and unspoilt a place as it is possible to find in a modern European country. Peaceful farms dot the countryside and, while the old fortified *bastides*, or walled towns, are a reminder of times when it was necessary to live within thick walls, there are also grand, beautiful houses and chateaux built in the eighteenth and nineteenth centuries. By the end of the twentieth century, many of these had fallen into decline, although a number are now being rescued by dedicated new owners.

One of these is the Château de Mail, not far from Auch: a classic house built probably in the late eighteenth century or the beginning of the nineteenth, on much older foundations. Americans Isabelle and Bob Higgins, both former actors, came from California to seek a complete life change.

The couple wanted a building with big, dramatic proportions in a house that had not been stylistically damaged, one with high ceilings, big windows and above all a "good flow" through the house and good interplay and access between house and garden. In 1990 they found the Château de Mail in a state of abandon. "It was the very last minute," says Isabelle Higgins. "The roof was collapsing and the water was coming in. If someone had not done something right then it would have been too late." Fortunately the exquisite plasterwork had not been seriously damaged, nor had most of the woodwork. On the other hand, features such as fireplaces had been removed long before.

It was a mammoth work of restoration: Bob and Isabelle threw their own skills and energy into it and, with the help of some excellent local

Left: The grey marble fireplace in the living room is a replacement found by the owners; the elaborate stucco-work around the mirror has also been carefully restored and regilded.

Above: In the main dining room the intricate plasterwork was regilded. The decorative alcoves at each side of the fireplace were created to replace cupboards.

Right: The simple French country dining table is matched with eighteenth-century chairs that are loosely covered in white linen. The floor is pine and has been sanded and treated to make it as pale as possible.

artisans, they have achieved a stunning result. A young and brilliant plasterer made moulds in cast iron of the original ceiling details and mirror frames and then recast the designs. The master-carpenter rebuilt almost the whole of the gracious staircase to the original design from a store of elm (now a rare wood) that Bob found on a nearby farm. The floors are unusual: on the ground floor they are pitch pine floorboards rather than parquet and upstairs squares of old poplar. All have been stripped and burnished by Bob to make them as pale as possible.

Once the structural and restorative work on original features was complete, Isabelle's blank canvas was ready and she was able to launch on her colour programme, which is the key to every-thing in this house. "I looked at the surrounding landscape with its very soft colour palette and I wanted to bring that colour range inside, so that the house would be complementary to its setting. I worked from room to room using the interplay of natural light and colour as a guide. The interior had to be an extension of the exterior – inside and outside in harmony." A guest arriving at the house at sundown may (weather permitting) have a dramatic illustration of what

Left: In the small second dining room, a sultane is decked with cushions and a hand-blocked red and gold shawl that was designed and made by Isabelle Higgins. Her fresco effects on the walls give a rich, Venetian effect.

Right: From an upstairs landing, doors open onto the bathroom with more hand-gilded plasterwork and a long white counter (just visible).

Below: Fresh flowers are an integral part of the décor at the Château de Mail.

she means. The main façade faces west and the wide entrance hall is thus suffused with late sunlight, which is answered by a deep, reddish gold on the inside walls overpainted with a barely discernible *trompe l'oeil* design of sumptuous curtains, to put some movement into the colour. "I wanted people to come into that big space and be filled with welcoming sunlight," says Isabelle.

She has painted every room following a similar philosophy, aiming to fuse light, colour and the room's purpose into an integrated whole. Experimenting as she went along, like a latter-day alchemist, sometimes reversing manufacturers' instructions, she used a wide range of different paints and paint effects, often mixing the colour with glaze to give a rich patina. There is a lot of very beautiful gilding in the house, emphasizing the rather Venetian style of the architecture. "Mail", the name of the house, can mean a number of things including "covered walkway" and this may be a reference to the Italianate arcade supported by delicate columns at the first floor level.

The layout of the house especially pleased Isabelle and Bob because there is a circular flow rather than a long *enfilade* of rooms that come to a dead stop at each end of the building. One can enter the grand hallway and walk through the main rooms, pass through the kitchen and

Below: Bob Higgins loves to cook, so the kitchen is an important room for him. It is large and high-ceilinged and the rich red walls are a symbol of nourishment. A massive wooden butcher's block sits on the two-tier table, and a collection of pots and pans hangs down from a rack for ease of use.

Right: The main entrance hall, where the elegant staircase had to be almost completely rebuilt to the original design by a master-carpenter, from a store of rare elm that Bob Higgins luckily found on a nearby farm. The faint trompe l'oeil *drape effect on the walls creates a feeling of movement.*

Above: Orchids punctuate a gilded bookcase in the dining room. The painted panels on the wall are part of Isabelle's design.

Above right: The bathroom has a basin sunk into a long counter. The gilded stucco around the mirror echoes that of the main rooms.

Left: This iron four-poster bed is a rare American import which Isabelle had extended to double its original size. Colours here are neutral to create a calm atmosphere for sleeping.

return to the starting point. From the hall, high double doors – present throughout the ground floor – lead to the living room, which faces east and thus gets the rosy pink light of early morning. A complementary décor echoes this: soft yellow with a pinkish touch on the walls and windows hung with pink and ecru silk curtains, which are designed so that panels of colour can be added or removed for a change of atmosphere. Deep red velvet cushions with a gold-printed design repeat the Venetian-Oriental touch that Isabelle loves; they are made in fabric designed and printed by her in the studio she has set up in one of the outbuildings.

Progress round the house continues into the main dining room, simply furnished with a French farm table surrounded by eighteenth-century chairs. Italianate glory is provided again by richly painted and gilded plasterwork around the mantle mirror and a glorious chandelier holding candles. Isabelle loves to see them all lit for dinner, and (a practical touch) uses a shield of chewing gum around the base of each candle to prevent wax dripping into the food. Bob is an excellent cook and the big Gascon kitchen is his favourite place in the house. The walls here are rich red for warmth and nourishment. Off the kitchen is a smaller, more intimate dining room, which has more gilding and a faint fresco effect on the walls, designed, Isabelle says, to look as if it were "very old and just disappearing". Upstairs the atmosphere changes – it is quieter. In the main bedroom, which contains a magnificent American wrought-iron bed, Isabelle has toned the colour down to neutrals. "It is all shadows – taupe on taupe and cream – a movement of shadows for sleeping."

Isabelle hopes to use the ideas she has worked out here to help others with their restoration projects. And there are still two floors left to do at the Château de Mail, not to mention the garden.

SEIGNEURIE DE PEYRAT

LUC AND BEATRICE VIENNET: LANGUEDOC

Left: The salon has high, elegant bookcases made from boiseries *(fine wood panelling) found in the attics. The original parquet floors are still intact in the main reception rooms.*

Right: Luc and Beatrice Viennet on the ornamental stone staircase that overlooks the gardens and vineyards.

Below: The ancient tower above the entrance gate is part of the remains of the fortifications of a much earlier house.

The coastal plain between Nîmes and Perpignan is the biggest vineyard area in the world. It was first planted by the Greeks in the sixth century BC around their port of Agde, then cultivated over a wider landscape by the Romans. Later it became very much the poor relation of the French wine industry, best known as the source of the rough reds that were distributed to farm and mine workers as a food supplement and regarded askance by the rest of the world. In recent years a quite remarkable revolution has taken place. Thanks to the influence of innovative wine makers from the "New World" – and to the dedication of some French producers – the Languedoc is now marketing wines of high quality.

The Languedoc is a vast swathe of country where wind and sun combine to create a very dry climate, but the region is still subject to terrible storms that cause frequent flooding. There is an epic beauty here due to the scale of the landscape and all it contains: the vast, open expanses of

the vineyards with the rows of vines marching into the distance like legionnaires; the cathedrals of Montpellier, Narbonne and Béziers looming out of their city centres as if to keep watch over the sea; the blue humps of the Cévennes to the north; and, on a clear day, the Pyrénées, visible on the southern horizon.

The important wine properties are correspondingly large. Luc and Beatrice Viennet live in and operate an ancient family *domaine* from a beautiful sprawl of ochreous buildings almost lost among their surrounding 200 hectares of vines, olives and *garrigue* (scrubland). "It is rather like a small village," explains Beatrice. She and Luc occupy the main house while Luc's mother lives in one wing and his aunt, the distinguished fine art curator Roselyn Bacou, keeps an apartment in another. The cellar and vineyard staff – among them some young Australian oenologists – have living space too.

Left and below: Sunlight dapples the back of the house, giving it a distinctly Mediterranean atmosphere.

As everywhere in this region, there are traces of great antiquity at here and originally there was probably some sort of Roman establishment on the site. What is certain is that a medieval building was enlarged and refurbished on a grand scale in the seventeenth century, surrounded by ornamental gardens and renamed Montplaisir. The most extravagant flourishes – mazes, aviaries and pavilions – have vanished leaving just the imposing but simple facade, which has a square tower at each corner and is embellished only by the ornate double staircase in carved stone at the centre. At the back there is a turreted entrance gate leading to a courtyard.

Right: The kitchen has high shelves decked with colourful Spanish ceramic plates. This decorative use of shelving to utilize the height of the room was copied from the kitchen at the Abbey of Fontfroide.

Left: The long corridor, with a marble floor, accommodates Beatrice Viennet's desk and her collection of ceramics by Didier Gardillou that is housed in matching dressers.

Right: The "big room" has a sixteenth-century carved wooden fireplace that was imported from the Château d'Isgny by Luc Viennet's grandmother. The curtain fabric is by Pierre Frey.

Above: A monumental ceramic wood-burning stove from Alsace has been installed in the "big room" to cope with heating such a large space.

Luc Viennet is the great-grandson of Gustav Fayet, a well-known artist, collector and patron who restored the Abbey of Fontfroide near Narbonne. Had he not bought that jewel of medieval architecture it would have been dismantled and taken stone by stone to the United States. The Seigneurie de Peyrat was part of Gustav Fayet's large estate, but when the Viennets came here in the mid-1980s it had not been inhabited for some time. Luc's family began to replant the vineyards and restructure the property – a massive task. "I had to learn to think big", says Beatrice, who is English and grew up on a pleasant farm near the Chequers estate, which her father managed. (As child she went to the Christmas parties held for Winston Churchill's grand-children and friends.) She was determined to import some English comfort to complement the French formality of her new home.

They were lucky, she says, in that most of the important structural work had been done by Luc's grandmother. This included recreating an important wooden ceiling – a *plafond à la française* – in the room that the Viennets call "*la grande pièce*", the big room, and installing a carved wooden Renaissance fireplace and marble floor. She had also had the parquet de Versailles floors in other main rooms restored.

From the big room there is access to the garden via the double staircase. A swathe of grass, dotted with terra-cotta jars brimming with purple bougainvillea and bordered by a stone balustrade, leads to the vineyards; a pine-clad hill beyond completes the view. A beautiful *allée* lined with alternately planted olive and cypress creates pleasing contrast of shape and colour. The size of the spaces defies ordinary gardening, although a pretty rose garden has just been planted. Beatrice wishes she could make a box garden, but it would have to be so big that it would take far too much time.

Inside, the rooms also have impressive volume, with a ceiling height of six metres and long windows which Beatrice has hung with curtains that introduce vivid colour. "I learned that in this climate with the intense light outside, strong colour inside is also necessary – too much brown furniture and dull tones can make it all very gloomy." She chose English fabrics from Colefax & Fowler and Geoffrey Bennison as well as fabric by Pierre Frey of Paris, and she used the Farrow & Ball colour chart. She was helped a lot by renowned interior designers Melissa Wyndham and Alidad Mahloudji, both of whom came from London to look at the place at the outset.

Above: The salon is furnished with French Louis XV furniture, which is covered in fabric from Colefax & Fowler. The curtains are by Pierre Frey, and the ceramics on the round table in the foreground are by Didier Gardillou.

For furnishings, Beatrice says, she had to make do with what was there – no great hardship – and what she could bring from her home in England. It all mixes well – for example, a Louis XV chair covered in English flowers rests on a Zeigler Turkish carpet with an unusual soft pink background that covers the French parquet. The kitchen is a long room that could have seemed like a corridor, but Beatrice has lifted the atmosphere by lining the high walls with shelves decked with bright Spanish plates, an idea she copied from the private kitchen at Fontfroide Abbey.

Beatrice worked for Sotheby's in London before coming to live in France and she is now their representative in the Languedoc. Initially an Oriental specialist, she has widened her scope. For her own pleasure she collects the work of ceramic artist Didier Gardillou and the long corridor that runs behind the reception rooms is enlivened by shelves of his brightly coloured pieces. There is still much to do, says Beatrice; two more floors to be exact. And in a corner of the courtyard there is a small chapel with an impressive cavalcade of larger-than-life saints painted in *grisaille* around the walls that is also awaiting restoration.

For the moment these projects will have to wait; updating the wine-production areas has had to take precedence. In another corner of the courtyard is the wine cellar, which includes a magnificent old kitchen that has been restored as a place from where to sell and celebrate the delicious varietal wines that Luc Viennet produces and that are part of the upgraded output that is so vital to the future of the Languedoc.

Below: A large, ornate gilt-framed mirror sits above the fireplace in the main bedroom. The fireplace is flanked by two comfortable Louis XV armchairs.

Right: The fabric headboards and curtains in the spare bedroom were made by Geoffrey Bennison. The landscape paintings were chosen from pictures already in the house.

CHATEAU de FAJAC

GENEVIEVE LEROY: LAURAGAIS

*Left: The main entrance hall
at the Château de Fajac,
showing the brick structure,
heavy wooden front door and
a portrait of a favourite cat.*

South of Toulouse is a no-man's-land, a landscape for so long part of the frontier struggles with Spain and between rival local factions that it seems somehow incurably depleted, an empty quarter. It is one of the most sparsely populated areas of France, and the inhabitants can be hard to spot; even the towering chain of the Pyrénées, the dominating emblem of the region, is elusive – often invisible in cloud or haze, then suddenly there, glittering and resplendent.

It is cold in winter on the open hills, scorching in summer, and famously windy, a land of fortress-castles and the ghosts of Cathar heretics, spectacular sunsets and wheeling birds of prey.

And yet the city of Toulouse grew rich on these quiet fields, now planted with sunflowers and other assorted workaday crops. At the interface of the Pays de Sault on the foothills of the mountains begins the fabled Pays de Cocagne, the land of plenty that rolls northeastwards of Toulouse towards Revel, Puylaurens and Albi, where an unassuming but precious plant with dark green leaves and yellow flowers – *isatis tinctoria* – was grown in abundance for centuries. From it was produced the precious blue dye known as *pastel* in French – woad or indigo in English. The only blue vegetable dye, which was once synonymous with affluence and luxury, *pastel's* cultivation and production was so commercially important that the whole region boomed. The land earned its soubriquet from the balls of mulched leaves known as *conques* or *cocagnes*, which in their day were worth more than gold.

Like most good things, the boom could not last: from the beginning of the sixteenth century a cheaper version of indigo came to Europe on the ships of the great East India Company, alongside pepper and cloves and other exotica, and the European woad industry began to decline. But, like the Cathars, the *pastelliers* left as a legacy their monuments, including palaces and some grandiose castles.

*Left: Geneviève Leroy
experiments with art in
rustic settings. She moved
to her chateau when it was
a near-ruin, and has
painstakingly restored it.*

*Below: The imposing red
brick façade of Fajac with its
heavy square towers. It was
built by a wealthy sixteenth-
century pastel merchant, who
later fell on hard times.*

One of these is the Château de Fajac-la-Relenque, a strange sixteenth-century edifice built in the red brick typical of the Toulouse area. (These bricks are thin, like large terra-cotta floor tiles, and are stacked with lime mortar to form thick, heat-retaining walls.)

Fajac's squat towers and rounded windows dominate the open countryside around it. In clear weather the mountains loom face-on at the front door. Bathed in mellow afternoon sunlight the building glows as if on fire, while in darker weather it can seem brooding and a little sad.

There is nothing brooding, however, about the present *châtelaine*, Geneviève Leroy, a Belgian art and antiques expert and valuer. She was working in Toulouse in the early 1990s when she noticed an advertisement in a small free newspaper for a "Napoleon III" (Victorian) chateau. When she went to have a look at it, she found it wasn't Napoleon III, but sixteenth-century. It had belonged to a *pastellier* who abandoned it when his fortunes declined, and almost nothing had been done to it for three centuries. The farmer who was trying to sell had considered pulling it down but the cost proved too high, and it had lain empty for the previous thirty years. Geneviève Leroy found it irresistible – "I have always been crazy about houses" – and moved in with her young family, including a six-week-old baby, to a home without windows, electricity or heating. "It was on a day of great cold and high wind. I must have been mad, but what is life without a little *folie*?"

Keen to oversee every aspect of the renovation, at first the family camped with the workers and set about the "calculated demolition" of nineteenth-century embellishments, such as ornate plasterwork, and little by little restored the chateau to a kind of skeletal glory. This is far from a full renovation, which would be impossible for one individual, but Geneviève has rescued the extraordinary shell of the building with its great rooms and monumental fireplaces and given it a new existence far removed from that of the merchant-farmers who built it.

Above: An arched window alcove with flowers in a pot on the tiled floor; a lamp in the wall niche and a colourful painted cupboard were found at a brocante *fair.*

Left: A coat of arms is hung askew as a sign of mourning. The hippopotamus skull is a relic of the owner's African childhood.

Above: The great "hall of honour" on the first floor. By stripping it back to the basic brick structure Geneviève has created a sense of warmth even in a huge room with large windows and minimal furnishings.

The house had been stripped of just about anything that could be moved; Geneviève recalls that all that remained was a badly damaged billiard table. The brick walls were crumbling in places, too, and what they could not restore they covered up with lime plaster. Just one plastered wall has been washed blue, Geneviève's tribute to *pastel*. Otherwise the walls provide the dominating colour, offset by a few pictures.

A limited central heating system was installed, but the main source of warmth was and is from the fireplaces, especially in the dining/living room adjoining the kitchen. A large wide table is placed close to the fire made of logs that are just slices of tree trunk. Here Geneviève's many guests and visiting artists sit and talk the night away, while the firelight flickers on the red brick walls, absorbing and radiating the warmth around them.

A relatively small kitchen was conceived as the cosy spot for winter, but Geneviève is not content with that. A huge unused space, the last "undone" room on the ground floor and at least 100 square metres, is in her sights as the future main kitchen. Making this will take time, and for the moment it is the principal playground for her twelve cats and kittens.

Left: Windows open to the sunshine of a summer day, but in winter the cold wind off the Pyrénées means that it is hard to keep warm, even by the enormous log fires.

Above: The dining room is the centre of life in the chateau. Visiting artists and friends often talk long into the night around the fireside table.

Right: Decorative artefacts and furniture that were found by Geneviève Leroy in local brocante markets.

Right: A four-poster bed in
cast-iron is draped in antique
white linen. The portrait of
an unknown lady is probably
eighteenth century. The
original beams, somewhat
corroded, have been lime-
washed white.

Left and below: The main
bedroom is the only place in
the chateau where the old
plaster remains intact on the
walls. Heavy linen sheets
have been used as bed
curtains; a built-in cupboard
has been stripped down.
The ceramic panther is
a recent arrival.

Once the walls were repaired and the floors were cleared, Geneviève decorated the house
with *objets trouvés*, a few pictures and little else. She was born and grew up in Africa and memen-
toes of that life include a hippopotamus skull in the salon. Beds are canopied with white linen;
chairs and tables and other furniture have been collected here and there.

As well as restoring her red elephant of a house, Geneviève has used her creative energy to
work with artists on community projects in the area: one involved fifteen artists showing their
work in the traditional *potagers* (vegetable gardens). "It is touching to see the young artists working alongside seventy-year-old gardeners," she says. Another project entailed dressing scarecrows
in *haute couture* clothes and planting them in the landscape. Geneviève works with the local
regional council on these and other ideas, and Fajac is also an informal place of retreat for artists
and writers who come to work and think – and talk around the huge fires.

PARIS CHIC
La Vie de Bohème

"We'll always have Paris", Humphrey Bogart tells Ingrid Bergman in a wistful moment in the movie *Casablanca*. The city continues to hold an indelible charm for foreign romantics and also for its own hard-headed people. Few cities inspire such passionate pride and strong sense of identification. It is, all agree, a great place to live and love.

Paris is a city of *quartiers*, urban villages roughly approximate to the twenty arrondissements. Each of these has a distinct character and atmosphere, and there seems to be an apartment – or at least an attic – for every taste and trade.

APARTMENT in FAUBOURG-SAINT-GERMAIN

CHARLOTTE MOSLEY

Left: A corner of the salon, showing the portrait of Nancy Mitford by Mogens Tvode (bottom left) and above, one of her sister, Diana Mosley, by the same artist. To the right, a drawing of Charlotte Mosley, editor of their letters, and above a painting by Drian.

Right: Charlotte Mosley on the sofa that Nancy Mitford once described as "utterly stunning, like a beautiful lady in a Dior dress for the first time". Visible through the doors behind is Charlotte's study, with another painting by Drian.

The upper reaches of the 7th arrondissement, also known as the Faubourg-Saint-Germain, form the grandest patch on the Rive Gauche, just across the Seine from the Louvre. The main thoroughfares, such as the rue du Bac, are lined with colourful galleries, antique and décor shops, cafés and restaurants, while the tall, sombre façades of the residential streets often hide imposing townhouses and secret gardens. On foot this area can sometimes seem stonily austere, but aerial views reveal this to be one of the greenest parts of Paris, hidden behind those towering *portes cochères*.

Very little here is modern unless you count Gae Aulenti's stunning revamp of the old Orsay railway station into one of the most famous art museums in the world. The refinement and elegance of the past glow from the windows of the exquisite *antiquaires*. Indeed, there are so many of these that they have their own annual festival – Le Carré Rive Gauche – during which the shops open late and serve champagne to the crush of couture-clad customers who come to look and buy. The area has a whiff of the *ancien régime* about it and is (they say) still so replete with aristocrats that in 1989 during the celebration of the 200th anniversary of the French Revolution a local baker put miniature guillotines instead of the usual little innocent favours into his *galettes des rois* (cakes traditionally served on Twelfth Night) just to outrage the duchesses among his clientèle.

Like all *quartiers* of Paris, Faubourg-Saint-Germain is something of a village in its own right, with a bustling street life and a range of shops selling delicious food and drink and other necessities. Artists and literati live here too, as if overspilling from the more intellectual 6th arrondissement, around nearby Saint Germain-des-Prés.

Charlotte and Alexander Mosley and their son, Louis, occupy a spacious apartment on the top floor of a solid nineteenth-century building not far from the Musée d'Orsay. They bought the flat in the late 1970s at the instigation of Charlotte's mother, who came over for the day from England and found it. It was a great bargain compared with anything available in London at the time.

Above: The salon has a happy mix of French formality and English comfort. Most of the furniture was inherited from different family houses.

Right: On the mantelpiece is a white porcelain clock given to Charlotte's grandfather by President Poincaré of France; a drawing of the Mosleys' son hangs over the mirror.

Far right: Diana Mosley's chaise longue covered in blue Toile de Jouy is to the right of the fireplace; a footstool in front of the fire is covered in fabric by John Stefanidis.

Left: An eighteenth-century
Italian giltwood mirror
reflects its twin on the
opposite side of the room;
the square-backed brown sofa
was owned by Nancy Mitford.

Below: The dining room was
decorated by John Stefanidis,
with wallpaper by Rubelli.
The 1950s chairs by Mrs
Mann of London were a
wedding present to Diana,
Lady Mosley, from Nancy
Mitford. The portrait is of
a Mosley ancestor.

"We had been looking for an attic", Charlotte says, "but this was irresistible, a wonderful place to live. What I loved at once was that it has a clear outlook on every side. The courtyard faces east and the kitchen and dining room have beautiful light in the morning. I loved all the old details, the window handles, the parquet and plasterwork."

John Stefanidis, an English designer and a great friend of the Mosleys, drew up the basic plans for the refurbishment. The work included renewal of the antique plumbing and wiring and total redecoration, a task done, bit by bit, over twenty years and which is still continuing.

Furniture was not a problem as most was culled from assorted family houses – Alexander's mother had sold a flat in Paris, while Charlotte's mother had sold a flat in London. They didn't have to buy anything except a bed.

This classic Parisian apartment has not been divided up as many others have been. It covers the whole floor of the building, and there are entrance doors on each side of the central stairwell so that you can walk through the front door, tour the flat and emerge from the kitchen.

The first impression is of warmth and a kind of inherent gaiety. While the flat is unmistakably French, there is an indefinably English ambience, giving it a more comfortable, lighter and less formal atmosphere than many similar Paris abodes.

70

The hall is wide and bright, and leads to a large salon with creaking parquet and a marble fireplace. The furnishings are elegant and eclectic, with inherited pieces jostling happily for dominance among other family treasures (such as the mantel clock given to Charlotte's grandfather, the Earl of Shaftesbury, by President Poincaré of France after the First World War), paintings, portraits and photographs.

Double doors that once led to the dining room now open onto Charlotte and Alexander's study, where they work side by side at computers on a vast table piled with papers and books. The walls are lined with bookcases made by Monsieur Thomas, a well-known local decorator.

When they moved to Paris, Alexander founded a publishing company and Charlotte worked with him. In the last decade, however, her career has taken off in another direction. Alexander is the son of the late Sir Oswald Mosley and Diana, Lady Mosley, one of the celebrated Mitford

Right: In the entrance hall there is a portrait of a family member dating back to the seventeenth century that was rescued from a house fire and restored. It hangs above a pretty eighteenth-century marble-topped console.

Left: The bed and window curtains are in Colefax & Fowler fabric.

Below: A pretty oval mirror hangs over the dressing-table with silver-gilt brushes.

Right: This bedroom used to be the dining room; the plate-warmer is an original feature.

sisters, and Charlotte's highly praised editions of the letters between her aunt-in-law Nancy Mitford and other members of that remarkable sisterhood have made her the keeper of an English legend. "Nancy was still alive when we came to Paris, but only just," says Charlotte. "She was already very ill and I met her only once."

Charlotte has since got to know Nancy very well on paper and also treasures some tangible relics. A poignantly elegant portrait, painted by the Danish artist Mogens Tvede, of Nancy in her own Paris flat hangs by the fireplace, placed as if to mirror one salon, one epoch to another. It was painted in 1947, soon after the publication of *The Pursuit of Love*, the first of Nancy Mitford's delicious trilogy of novels that both mocked and romanticized her own English upper-crust family and the French *beau monde* that she frequented in Paris.

Nancy's yellow Louis XVI sofa is here too, a perfect symbol of the society she inhabited in France, although she brought it from England. Charlotte explains: "Lady Redesdale – Nancy's mother, 'Muv' to the family and in the novels – had admired the sofa, which belonged to one of Lord Redesdale's tenant farmers. The farmer's wife left it to her in her will and it went to Nancy after Muv's death. Nancy had it re-covered in yellow silk damask and wrote to Diana that it 'looks utterly stunning, like a beautiful lady in a Dior dress for the first time'."

Diana's *chaise longue*, covered in blue *Toile de Jouy* and brought from a former home in Ireland, sits across the room like an equally elegant but very different sister.

APARTMENT IN MONTMARTRE

VALERIO ADAMI

Left: The main living area of the apartment is dominated by the dark geometry of a chair by Charles Rennie Mackintosh. The highly polished black-tiled floor is softened by a Chinese carpet.

Right: Valerio Adami, Italian artist and collector, who now only visits his second home in Paris occasionally, still regards the city as a source of inspiration.

From all across Paris, even in the depths of the narrowest streets, there are myriad vantage points from where to catch surprise glimpses of the opulent white basilica of Sacré-Coeur, perched in glory on the summit of the Butte de Montmartre, gleaming in the sun and beckoning as to a palace in some distant kingdom. And arriving in Montmartre does feel like reaching somewhere quite separate: it clings to the highest of the Paris hills (129 metres) and looking down can feel like floating above the city. At the same time, the popular, Hollywoodesque image of Paris is largely derived from this series of interlinked hamlets, steep stairways and lampposts, leafy little lanes and gardens, cottages and cobbled streets, vineyards, windmills, bookstalls, cabarets and tiny restaurants.

Montmartre has guarded its distinct identity with pride – the inhabitants once even declared it an independent republic – and it has always also been a sacred place of pilgrimage. The name probably derives from "Mount of Martyrs", since Saint Denis and his friends were supposedly executed here, although there are more profane interpretations; during the Revolution it was briefly renamed Mount Marat, after the revolutionary leader. Sacré-Coeur was built in an extravagant Byzantine style in the 1880s by public subscription, in expiation of the sins of Parisians under the Commune of 1870, which was seen as a godless, illegal government. It has since become one of the most popular and emblematic monuments of Paris, a favourite subject for painters and attracting so many tourists that buses are now banned at the weekends and in the evenings.

From the mid-nineteenth century, Montmartre was a lure to artists, writers, actors, poets and composers, attracted by the (then) low cost of living and the quality of air and light. After the First World War the Bohemians decamped to Montparnasse, but the historic roll call remains. Composer Eric Satie began his career in a Montmartre cabaret; Picasso, Salvador Dali, Picabia, Braque, Apollinaire and film director Buñuel among many others lived here at one time or another, and the romantic Cimetière de Montmartre contains the remains of François Truffaut, Berlioz and Offenbach, Fragonard and Dégas, Théophile Gautier, Alexandre Dumas *fils* and Stendhal, physicist Foucault and the dancer Nijinsky.

Italian artists Valerio and Camilla Adami follow in this long tradition, living the winter months in a spacious apartment at the top of an early twentieth-century building tucked behind Sacré-Coeur. They came to Montmartre simply because they liked it very much. They were living elsewhere in Paris: Camilla had had a serious operation and their apartment was not ideal to work in, so they began searching. When Valerio found a dead pigeon on the balcony of their old flat and on that same day a nest of tiny live baby pigeons on the balcony of one he was look-ing at, he saw it as a sign that he should take it immediately. "I think houses do have certain atmospheres and are capable of bringing happiness or otherwise," he says. (Salvador Dali lived in the same street for a time and, after some research, Adami is almost certain that it was in his apartment or the one above. Whether Dali was happy there or not history does not relate.)

The Adamis redecorated throughout, moving existing wood panelling from one part of the apartment to another and converting a former music room into Valerio's *atelier*, where he works every day. Afternoons are sacred: "No one comes in here between two and eight," he says. "Once you start on a journey like that you need to follow where it takes you; ideas do not develop otherwise."

In the main living room a few chosen pieces, including chairs by Le Corbusier, Mackintosh and in the Bauhaus style, are entirely harmonious with the flat's elegant design, and the effect is uncluttered, precise and restful. The floor is polished to a shining black; the walls are white;

Above: Adami's studio, with work in progress. He paints and thinks here in the afternoons.

Right: The wall panel is called "Latrine in Times Square" and was painted by Adami in New York in 1968. In the foreground is an early twentieth-century Chinese carpet.

Left: The painting is by the Chilean artist, Matta; fabric in a Bauhaus design covers the sofa; the decorative Indian cushions are covered in fabric by Asha Savahaba. The white column and the window with panes reminiscent of a Japanese screen were added when the Adamis redesigned the apartment.

Above: A round window with an impressive view of Sacré-Coeur, with a Senufo wood-carving from the Ivory Coast outlined against it.

79

and a large window with a rectangular black frame is reminiscent of a Japanese paper screen. It looks out on to what Adami calls "that picture postcard view" of the Basilica, charmingly semi-obscured by a large tree. The Adamis had trouble getting permission for the window. They discovered an agreement between the building and the convent opposite preventing the installation of windows. Eventually work was able to go ahead after a loophole was found in the agreement, although the architect made sure that the window remained faithful to the style and period of the building. It seemed logical to continue the interior décor in the same vein.

Valerio Adami has led a nomadic life. He was an artist from an early age ("I was painting even in my mother's stomach. It was graffiti then," he says). Studying with the Russian painter Oskar Kokoschka at the age of fourteen was a formative and inspirational experience that marked him very deeply. He returned to study in Milan and moved on to London and then Paris, from where he has travelled on many expeditions to South America, notably to Venezuela and Mexico.

Left: An elegant spiral staircase leads to the upper floors of the apartment. The leather sofa has cushions in Bauhaus-style fabric. The two chairs in the foreground are by Le Corbusier. A sculpture by Chilean artist Inès Vega stands against the window.

Above: The dining area features a high-backed semi-circular chair in lacquered oak by Charles Rennie Mackintosh. It is similar to one made for the cashier in the Willow Tea Rooms, Glasgow, in 1904. Some of Adami's collection of twentieth-century pictures are on the wall or propped against it. The large rustic ceramic plates on the table are from the Dolomites.

Adami also kept a studio in New York for eighteen years and has another in India, where he goes every January to recharge his spiritual and creative batteries. The walls of the Montmartre apartment are decorated with works of art that Adami has "met" during his travels, including drawings by Miró, Giacometti, Matta, Alechinski, Dufy and Steinberg, plus a collection of eighteenth-century drawings. Adami says that he is not so much a collector as someone who develops a rapport with an object and acquires it for that reason. "One develops an affinity with that object, one has to love it. It is better, I think, to be an amateur in that sense than a professional." The apartment itself has influenced his collection. "It won't let me put just anything in it, it will reject anything that is not in keeping with the style. My Italian house by Lake Maggiore, on the other hand, has been designed specifically to accept anything I decide to put in it, whether it be kitsch or unsuitable or clashing or whatever."

The Adamis do not spend as much time in Montmartre as they once did: they also have a house in Monaco and Adami works a lot in Italy, notably on opera set design, as for a 2003 production of *The Flying Dutchman* at the San Carlo Theatre in Naples. But Paris is the place that has given him the most and is where he works best, so he always returns here.

STUDIO IN MONTPARNASSE

VICTOR KOULBAK

*Left: The corner of the living
room in Victor Koulbak's
studio. The creative clutter is
in fact a carefully arranged
and inspirational composition.*

*Right: Victor Koulbak,
an artist who escaped the
old regime in Russia to
live in happy exile in
Montparnasse.*

*Below: One of the artist's
collection of busts: this one,
which looks like Lorenzo de
Medici, is of a young
Florentine nobleman of
the Renaissance period.*

Montparnasse, in the 14th arrondissement, is not as picturesque as some of the prettier *quartiers* of Paris, but it has long been the haunt of artists and writers, craftsmen and scholars. Towards its most southern point, where the main roads that radiate south out of Paris snake together into the *péripherique*, lies the green hill of the Parc Montsouris (the name translates quaintly as Mouse Mountain), with its lawns, exotic trees and old-fashioned merry-go-round.

The Cité Internationale Universitaire de Paris, founded in the 1920s for foreign students in the spirit of the Latin Quarter's medieval colleges, flanks the park with pavilions built by different nations. There are thirty-five of them in wildly varying styles of architecture, from the geometric Dutch pavilion designed by Dudok in 1928, to the Swiss house built on stilts, or *pilotis*, in 1932 by Le Corbusier. Bordering this campus to the west lies Montrouge Cemetery, overlooked by an imposing 1920s housing development in red brick and white stucco, standing seven floors high around two courtyards. At the top of one of these blocks, in the most urban of settings, the Russian artist Victor Koulbak has created a rustic hideaway, a cosy home and studio.

Koulbak was born in Moscow in 1946 and grew up during the grim twilight of the Stalinist régime. As a child he shared one room with his parents, an uncle and his sister in an apartment that housed seven other families. To escape, he drew obsessively from an early age on any scrap of paper he could lay hands on.

When he won a place at the USSR Academy of Art, the young Koulbak found himself involved in a secret war against the communist régime: forbidden ideas and books were exchanged, and students were often taken to see banned paintings hidden away in museum cellars. Colluding teachers played along with the offical line by warning of the decadence of religious art but then going on to speak of its beauty.

Koulbak later worked as a draughtsman for publishing houses while continuing to paint and draw, but decided to leave Russia

after several of his exhibitions were closed for being anti-Soviet. "I couldn't work like that," he says mildly. To his surprise, even after he had taken part in a famous show in 1974 when the KGB attacked the artists and burned their works, he obtained an exit visa. He went to Sweden, then to Paris, bringing only a few things with him, including some small icons that belonged to his family.

It is hard to believe that this gentle, elegant man clad in English tweeds and polished Lobb shoes has had such a fiery and painful past, but a steely commitment to his ideals shines through his reserve. Because of his overcrowded early life, having his own private space is of primordial importance. It took him many years to find the perfect apartment-cum-studio in Paris but when he saw his current home he knew it was right.

Above: The living room, where some of Victor Koulbak's copies of the works of the great masters are displayed on the walls. "They have so much to teach", he says.

There are three main rooms: a sitting room, a bedroom (originally one large space before the previous owner put up a dividing wall) with a staircase up to the studio. Koulbak needed to make his surroundings conducive to his work and rearranged the apartment much as he plans his paintings, designing every detail himself. Colours are mostly whites, greys and browns, tones echoed in his own exquisite silverpoint drawings that recall the fifteenth- and sixteenth-century works that inspire him. There is a rich blue in the dining area and a muted fresco-like colour on the walls, which he achieved, in his words, by "incident effect". When he started stripping off the hideous wallpaper there were stubborn scraps of paper and a lot of glue underneath that he couldn't remove. The paint wouldn't go on evenly and so, using his knowledge as a painter rather than as a decorator, he worked around it and created a sort of distempered effect. "I would never do it again, it was

Below: The artist saved these few travelling icons that belonged to his family when he left Russia. Preserving them was of great importance to him: "Such treasures were being used as firewood," he says.

Right: On the writing table is a reproduction of a detail from a famous Michelangelo sculpture (the head of one of the sons of Laocoon), and a small bird cage of the kind in which ortolans (buntings) are fattened for a gourmet's table.

Right: A display of objects that Victor Koulbak has collected in flea markets over the years. The blue wall was painted to look like an aged fresco that has been exposed to the elements.

Left and below: Victor Koulbak's studio was inspired by Fra Angelico's famous Annunciation painting. "The goal is to create beauty", the artist says.

a nightmare," he says, laughing. He even painted on more glue and scratched up the surface on the smoother areas so that the effect would be continued. The look is textured and aged, very much like fresco that has been exposed to the elements. He deliberately left patches rough and unfinished – "I didn't want to make it perfect."

In the high, light studio with views to the limits of Paris, bright flowers grow from birdcages, and an arched wooden balcony inspired by Fra Angelico's *Annunciation* fills one wall. Koulbak's copies of drawings by Michelangelo, Pisanello, Raphael, Dürer and others hang on the walls, echoing the training he had in Moscow, when he spent much time copying and replicating old masters. "The best way to learn is to copy," he maintains. "I could never put my own work on the walls. The great artists have so much to teach us and I shall never stop learning. The painter, to my mind, is a craftsman who creates a beautiful object. The goal is

to create beauty – I cannot understand why people choose to live without beauty, without that everything is pointless."

The *objets* in the apartment have been trawled from flea markets and found on Koulbak's travels. "I am not a collector," he says. "That requires some sort of systematic approach, whereas when I see something that appeals to me it's a kind of magic. It becomes a question of 'that's mine' and I have to have it. For this reason I don't allow myself to go to flea markets any more. I can never come away empty-handed and I can't get rid of things once I have them, they become part of the family; so if I carried on I would be overwhelmed."

He speaks often of his "family" of artefacts and there is a kind of harmony in the diverse assembly of busts, daggers, dried flowers, boxes and pictures. Most remarkable are the carved barley sugar columns topped by Corinthian capitals that he found in Budapest and the travelling icons covering one wall. It is especially important to him that such treasures are kept and looked after, since he saw so much destruction in Russia, where icons were even used as firewood.

Above: The bedroom is tiny but well-stocked with a mix of religious and decorative objects. The painting over the bed is Victor Koulbak's copy of a Leonardo drawing.

His furniture is pine, both Swedish and Spanish, which he likes because the eye makes a direct contact with the surface of the wood as it is, warm-toned and worn. "You only have to put wax on it once in a while and I love the smell of wax; I like simple things." Two old Persian rugs lie on the unvarnished wooden floor. The leather armchair is scratched and battered, but extremely comfortable. "I don't have a country house, so I created my country house here," he says.

The apartment has perhaps the atmosphere of an old Russian dacha, a personal haven full of memories.

These days Koulbak spends most of his time in Malta where the light is better and there is fifteenth- and sixteenth-century art and architecture to inspire him. But looking around his Paris aerie he says that there is nothing he could part with. He comes back often to commune with them and to sell his portraits. "All my drawings are portraits, whether of an apple, a bird or a man."

Right: The bust of a Florentine lady seems to rise from an armoire with a selection of religious and domestic artefacts around her. To the right is one of a pair of Hungarian eighteenth-century spiral mahogany columns that mark the divide between living and dining areas. The chair came from a charity shop.

LOFT IN BELLEVILLE

DJAMILA TAULE

Left: The uncluttered, high space of the ground floor showroom serves as a blank canvas for designer Djamila's ideas. The décor changes constantly to reflect work in progress on a collection.

Right: Djamila with her dalmatian, Walter. She knew when she saw the old, disused warehouse that it would be perfect as a home for herself and for the development of her fashion business.

There is a different rhythm of life in Belleville, the somewhat fancifully named part of the 20th arrondissement in the northwest of the city. A chaotic and colourful area with a highly disparate, multi-racial population and an unstressed, almost Mediterranean ambience, it feels as if certain streets have been borrowed from Marseille. Large numbers of North African immigrants live here, alongside people from former French colonial Africa and more recent arrivals from Eastern Europe. Threaded through the ethnic mix are the new young high-achieving Parisians, making their way in fashion and design, media or the music business.

Belleville was once, incredibly, a pretty medieval village surrounded by vineyards. In the eighteenth century Parisians came up here to drink a glass of wine (cheaper than in the highly taxed city centre) known as a *guinget*. From this developed a whole kingdom of *guinguettes*, little bars, or café-gardens and cabarets, where people came to relax and dance on Sundays. In the 1860s Belleville began to fill up with the overflow of workers and paupers displaced by Haussmann's great clearance of the city centre to make way for his *grand boulevards* and bourgeois apartment blocks, and the district declined into one of the worst slum areas. The refugees brought their tough revolutionary traditions with them, however, and this was the last stronghold of the Paris Commune in 1871. The area later suffered the well-meaning but not always happy attentions of twentieth-century utopian architects and redevelopers, resulting in the construction of many modern tower blocks. Now, young trendsetters buying up cheap properties are reviving the older buildings.

Djamila Taulé, with her label "d j a m" is one of the young rising stars in the Paris fashion world. She bought her enormous Belleville loft at a bargain price in the late 1990s, in an ancient form of auction sale known as a *vente à chandelles*, in which the notary lights three candles and the person who bids last before the third candle goes out is the winner. The word "loft" has been borrowed from English to mean any former industrial space; Djamila's was a disused factory depôt with three storeys, the ground floor offering the biggest space, with a very high ceiling

Left: In the vast ground floor room, Djamila mixes all sorts of styles. The high-tech "Tour Eiffel" table with riveted corners by American artist Adam has Oriental chairs from Veranda in Trouville around it. The cushions are covered in Vietnamese fabric.

Right: The ground floor looking towards the kitchen area to the left under the stairs, with sitting and dining areas within easy reach. The bronze sculpture in the foreground is by Compain.

Below: Long shot of the room, which is sometimes used as an exhibition space. Pictures by Djamila's father Antoni Taulé hang on the walls; the painted metal beams and concrete floor recall the building's past.

and skylights. She admits that she came for the building and its price, not to be in Belleville: "I didn't like the area at all", she recalls, "but I just blanked it out when I saw this space because it exactly suited what I was looking for." Before this she lived in another loft in the expensive Marais district, but it became too small to accommodate d j a m's growth.

Here the scale is so different that Djamila had to buy completely new furniture; what she had would have been wrong, too *rikiki* (stingy), she says. She has stamped her own style, or non-style – she does not stop to reflect on what she is putting together – on the white space of the ground floor showroom that also serves as a blank canvas for her ideas. The décor changes

Left: An antique mantelpiece gives the private sitting room a focal point; the figures are from the flea market and the flowered fabric is by Dominic Picquier.

Right: The tall factory windows and vaulted brick ceiling give light and warmth to the sitting room. The cast iron chair is from the flea market and the square table from Veranda. Paintings are by Antoni Taulé.

regularly, to reflect the collection being worked on by a team beavering away at tables dotted around the far end of the room, drawing up designs and dealing with sales and enquiries.

Enormous sofas fill a living area at the other end of the space. One side of the wall is painted pink, but this will soon change as Djamila has become tired of it. Likewise, the objects and furniture that she finds at flea markets and *depôts de vente* tend only to stay a while before being replaced by something new that has caught her eye. "I'm not materialistic but if I like something I tend to get it without even thinking if it will fit in or not. As a result I have lots of things that don't go together. The result is a bit chaotic, but I quite like that, it feels alive," she says. Her taste leans towards the baroque, in the sense of warm colours and strong shapes: "I suppose I am trying to recreate something that reminds me of warm southern places and the sun; I like wood and things that you can live with, I can't bear those very décor kinds of places with chrome and shiny kitchens."

Above: The bathroom is one of the designer's favourite places. She created the double washstand by putting porcelain basins into an old kitchen table.

Left: The oval acrylic bathtub is placed in the centre of the room, just at the top of the stairs. Candles and flowers enhance the atmosphere.

Upstairs are her private quarters and her favourite rooms – the bedroom and bathroom, places where her most intimate possessions are kept. She likes to live lying down and really loves her bed and her bath. The bed, a modern version of a four-poster, is by Henri Quinta. The bath is her *pièce de resistance* and a lot of thought went into the choice. A stone tub was considered but it weighed a ton, then a large wine barrel/vat, which would have been fun but impossible to keep really clean. She wanted something designed by Philippe Starck, which was too expensive, but she found almost the same model from a big bathroom store, the only difference being the price and that it is in plastic rather than metal. Djamila liked the idea of having an open bathroom and bedroom space and positioned her glamorous tub in the middle of the open floor, because it amused her and shocked some of her friends.

The daughter of artist Antoni Taulé and descended on her mother's side from Marshal Ney, Napoleon's "bravest of the brave", Djamila has always loved art and fashion. She studied textile and fashion at the LISAA, L'Institut Supérieur des Arts Appliqués, before going on to spend many internships at various couture houses. In 1994 she entered a competition for design students and won as a prize a free stand at the Fashion Festival in Hyères on the Côte d'Azur.

*Left: Djamila's bedroom,
with early twentieth-century
kelim on the floor, built-in
wardrobes and two comfy
chairs. The eighteenth-century*
bergère *(right) came from
her mother and is covered
in fabric by Dominique
Picquier; the other chair
came from a* brocante.

*Right: The four-poster bed
is in solid pine by Henri
Quinta for Campagne
Première. The silk quilted
bedcover is Vietnamese.
Voile curtains shield the light
from the large windows.*

For that she designed the first d j a m collection, which was highly successful. She started her company and now sells her clothes in young, clever Paris boutiques and to Japan, Italy and Hong Kong. Djamila prefers to work in natural materials, producing her own mixes, developing an ongoing interest in textiles. She likes rough, unrefined fibres – cotton most of all – disliking silk as being "much too slippy".

She travels a lot, but always to the same places: Normandy, Formentera, Switzerland and the mountains. Invariably she brings back some treasure trove, especially antique linen and lace sheets, but she does not like getting attached to things as it makes her anxious; she wants the freedom to get up and go tomorrow if she feels like it. "That's why everything changes, it gives a good sense of going forward, not getting stuck." One day Djamila will leave Paris to go in search of sun and warmth, probably in Marseille. Belleville is just the first stop.

APARTMENT in LE SENTIER

DIMONAH AND MEHMET IKSEL

Left: The apartment is a sumptuous arbour of peace, entirely decorated with the beautiful painted panels that the Iksels import from India.

Right: Mehmet and Dimonah Iksel met in Jaipur, India; their common love of Oriental design and materials has been the foundation of a thriving business.

The district known simply as *Le Sentier*, in the 2nd arrondissement, is the hub of the capital's rag trade and traditionally one of the liveliest – and noisiest – in Paris. Wholesale and retail operations provide work here for the city's 75,000 tailors and seamstresses, feeding garments to the cheap clothing shops in Les Halles and the boutiques around the Place des Victoires alike.

Once an almost completely Jewish quarter – peopled by successive waves of immigrants from Eastern Europe, Germany, the Middle East and Africa – the Sentier has latterly become one of the most ethnically diverse parts of the city. Chinese, Turks, Serbs and Greeks have arrived to fill some of the sad space left by the thousands of Jews – perhaps half the local population – who were deported by the Nazis during the Occupation. But the trade is still the same and the clatter of trucks unloading bales of cloth early in the morning and the crush of the workforce making for home in the evening continues, while falafel and kebab houses jostle for customers.

It is not a rich district, but it touches on grandeur. The rue Chabanais, where Dimonah and Mehmet Iksel live with their two sons, Kublai and Sinbad, and their Turkish Van cat Isabelle, runs close to the Palais Royal with its long arcades and beautiful enclosed formal gardens built for Richelieu in the seventeenth century. During the Revolutionary period it belonged to the renegade Duc d'Orléans, the king's cousin, and gambling houses and bordellos flourished under its arcades. It also became a hotbed for sedition and political ferment: it was here, on an upturned wine barrel, that Camille Desmoulins called for citizens to take arms and march on the Bastille. Garment workers were in the ensuing fray that changed history.

The Palais Royal now houses the Council of State and the Ministry of Culture, and its highly desirable apartments are among the most expensive in the city. The Bank of France and the Bourse are nearby, as is the flamboyant Opéra, built by Charles Garnier in the nineteenth century. But just around the corner in the Sentier some of the old louche life survives. "The area

Left: A collection of objects that the Iksels have brought back from their travels to India and from the Paris flea markets.

also now has the highest concentration of *échangeiste* [transvestite] clubs," says Mehmet. "But it's all very discreet."

The Iksels love living here, having moved from Saint-Germain on the Left Bank, which they found had become too full of tourists. Dimonah chanced to see a billboard advertising the rue Chabanais apartment for rent. "As soon as we saw the flat we fell in love with it – and managed to negotiate a cheaper price as we couldn't afford it, but really wanted it," says Mehmet.

The apartment, on the first floor – the *étage noble*, with high ceilings and long windows – of an eighteenth-century house, is primarily their home, but also doubles as a showroom for the beautiful painted panels they import from India. It is spacious and tranquil, a sumptuous arbour of peace, with the delicate tones and patterns of the art filling every available inch of wall space in the two main living rooms. Delicate, jewel-hued images of trees and plants are interspersed with richly ornamented figures and Islamic abstract patterns, with touches of antique gilt catching the light here and there. The feeling is rather like entering a palace from *The Thousand and One Nights*, with a soft golden light reflecting off the panels and suffusing everything.

Mother-of-pearl inlaid boxes with exquisitely intricate patterns adorn the tables and the fabrics on the comfortable furniture arranged in small groups throughout both rooms echo the rich brocaded fabrics and damasks. Kilims and rugs cover the floor, potted plants and a palm tree add a green touch to enhance the elegant airy feel, and a backdrop of rich draped curtains frames the four-metre-high windows.

Right: The lofty ceilings of the eighteenth-century drawing room have made a perfect gallery for the Indian painted panels. The green of the palm and other potted plants makes the room seem like an enchanted garden.

Left: The opposite end of the large drawing room (see page 103), showing the Rubelli curtains that Dimonah bought in an auction for a song. The floor is covered with kilims and richly coloured Oriental rugs.

Below: Between the high windows is a series of exquisite panels. Hand-painted with elaborate medallions, they originate from India.

Mehmet is the son a Turkish career diplomat and his childhood was spent in several places, notably Greece, where his father was ambassador, and then Bonn, where signing the Adenauer agreements on immigration meant, he says dryly, that his father was responsible for the three million Turks living and working in Germany today. Given the choice of living in London or Paris when he left Oxford, he says that, "Paris was just so beautiful and on the right scale; London I found depressing." Iksel *père* was also a collector of rugs and books, and had an interest in archaeology, which inspired in the young Mehmet a love of beautiful things, reflected in the eclectic choice of decorative objects and beautiful carpets and kilims in the apartment.

Dimonah, half-Hungarian, half-Iraqi, whose family moved to the United States when she was young, formerly worked in jewellery design and creation. The couple met in Jaipur in the late 1980s: she was on holiday and he was travelling on business buying miniatures, and they quickly discovered a mutual love of applied and decorative arts. Between them they developed the idea of training Indian painters to work up designs and paint them onto large panels that could then be used as wall décor or stand alone as paintings. Dimonah was also inspired by the beautiful painted wallpapers she had seen in Italy. The couple set up a workshop in Jaipur and spent the first few years experimenting with different designs and styles until, by trial and error and much research, they came up with the notion of reworking classical and Oriental designs and figurative works. The stunning results can be seen on their walls and are sold round the world by catalogue and on the internet.

Mehmet does detailed research for each design, working from historical prints, and often going to consult the extensive collections housed at the Bibliothèque Nationale just down the road. "I love Islamic and oriental art and ceramics," he says, "especially from the Mogul, Ottoman and Persian periods, although I am also fascinated by Japanese textiles and the work that was produced in North Africa, Spain and Egypt."

The Iksels work with top designers from America and Europe, although they have never gone mainstream or into mass production. However, they are now working on the production of high-quality prints of their designs from digital images so that they can make the pictures more accessible, and share their love and knowledge of good decorative art.

They do not collect original pieces as they are too expensive, but then, as Mehmet says, a piece does not have to be expensive to be beautiful. They find objects in obscure corners of the Drouot salerooms nearby or the Paris flea markets. They also make their own pieces, especially furniture. Recently Demonah has begun seeking out small pieces of furniture, tables in particular, and lacquering them. Druout has offered some stunning bargains, such as a set of silk Rubelli curtains which went for "nothing" and exactly fitted their high windows.

It all looks very permanent but soon will vanish, as they plan to take down the panels next year and replace them with frescoes with an oriental feel, especially using the tile designs from Isnik in Turkey. Part of the point of the panels is that they can be taken down easily, sold or moved to another home. Fresco is more permanent.

Mehmet and Dimonah are unashamed traditionalists. "I like modern art very much", says Mehmet, "but I'd rather not have to live with it in my house and look at it every day. What we do is easier to live with. People come in and see this and are astonished by what a few paintings can do for their interiors."

Left: The library houses the Iksels' impressive collection of books on Oriental art and design. A lacquered chest, set against more Indian panels, and a comfortable sofa covered in a rich silk brocade complement the sumptuous décor.

Right: The Iksels also make and decorate some of their furniture. The small octagonal table here was lacquered by Dimonah. The embroidered cushions are Indian. A tall palm adds a fresh touch of green.

APARTMENT ON THE RIVE GAUCHE

AGNES COMAR

Left: The entrance hall in Agnès Comar's apartment has a minimalist polished concrete staircase with cast-iron bannister; the floor is in cobblestones like the courtyard outside. The 1950s chandelier is by Bagès.

Right: Agnès Comar, a restless designer who uses her own homes as laboratories for her decoration ideas before moving on.

The public face of central Paris changes little, which is one of its great charms. There are strict controls about what a private citizen can do to the exterior of an ancient building, but within the tight corset of the classic structures, bold designs can often be found. This is a city of celebrated decorators – Olivier Gagnaire, Andrée Putman, Philippe Starck, Jacques Grange and many, many others – who have wrought wonders inside small apartments, grand *hôtels particuliers* (private townhouses) and chic restaurants alike endowing Paris with an evolving glamour. Their more avant-garde ideas and *outré* experiments cause controversy when seen too publicly, but Parisians, who have a strong sense of the theatrical, tend to admire a good stylish marriage between old stones and new clothes.

Agnès Comar is one of the most sought-after designers and decorators of the new century. A veritable sorceress with colour, she has played her favourite, vivid hues – purples, deep shades of red and orange, acid green – magically against the sober background of ancient grey stone in her most recent Paris apartment. It is situated on the ground floor of an eighteenth-century *hôtel particulier* in one of the most fashionable streets of the 7th arrondissement. At the entrance, massive double doors suggest that an antique interior in keeping with the period of the tall, heavy building lies on the other side. They open to reveal a wide, square courtyard with well-clipped and rounded bay trees amid seams of wild grasses sown between cobblestones. Often such courtyards are perforce taken over as parking lots, with ivy and other wall climbers the only green relief; here is a welcome touch of the countryside in the city.

Agnès Comar's apartment is built around three sides of this secret garden; the building has been faced with a continuous glass extension to enlarge the living area and to create something of a penthouse effect at ground level. The designer has worked with her architect daughter, Anne-Cécile, to transform what was nothing but a run-down clutter of old storehouses. There is sense of continuity from garden to house as the long front entrance hall is also cobbled and, like the rest of the apartment, seems like an almost seamless extension of the exterior.

Above: The voilages *and*
drapes in the apartment all
come from Agnès Comar's
own collection of household
linens and fabrics.

Left: The main living area
is treated as an extension of
the garden. The light from
the glass roof is softened by
panels of cotton voile by
Agnès Comar. The 1950s
armchairs by Jansen are
covered in raw silk from
Yves Gastou. The rug is
in woven abaca.

Right: The same room, with
a clear view of the elegantly
folded silk window curtains,
hung to give a view of the
courtyard and its terra-cotta
pots beyond.

Inside the hall, an ultramodern concrete stairway with a simple metal handrail leads to bed-rooms upstairs, and a tribal skirt is hung as an artefact on the wall, offset by a long, dappled cabinet and a crystal chandelier, both from the 1950s.

In the salon, which has a cobbled floor like the garden and the entrance hall, the glass roof is hung with swathes of fine pale cotton voile designed by Agnès Comar; this idea is repeated throughout the apartment to soften the glare in the "glasshouse" rooms. There is a discernible Japanese influence in the furnishings – Agnès Comar works a great deal in Japan and the United States and she has no hesitation about mixing styles and ideas, taken from wherever she finds them. There are also many pieces from the 1950s and 1960s, periods the designer much admires.

Habitually she uses her own living quarters as a laboratory for her ideas. "I do not live in my houses for long; once they are finished, *paf!*, I get rid of them and move on," she says. It is rather

Above left: Heavy glass vases hold flowers in front of the first of a line of mirrors in the dining room.

Above: A long banquette sofa reinforces the linear layout of the apartment.

Right: Two tables laid end-to-end fill the dining space.

Left: Another view of the staircase, with a 1970s cabinet covered in ponyskin. The standard lamp is by Agnès Comar.

like striking a theatrical set, except that she leaves it behind for someone else to enjoy. This apartment is number twelve in the series.

A tiny, elegant woman clad in the rich colours that she knows so well how to combine, Agnès Comar appears like part of her own décor. As she walks through the apartment she adjusts a hanging here, corrects a lamp there. Nothing is left to chance, nothing must be out of place. Here is great flair and startling originality, but under a tight rein, with nothing serendipitous or haphazard.

The squared-off "u" shape of the apartment creates a rather narrow, linear effect. Rooms lead straight from one to another, and Agnès Comar has solved this problem by "going with it"

Above: Pretty pink and red rose petals in a 1960s ceramic dish under the stairs.

Right: A "gangway" bridge at the upper level is a continuation of the staircase and links two bedrooms. Large framed antiquarian architectural plans fill the walls of the stairwell.

Left: In the main bedroom the bed is a mattress on a platform. The bed linen, cover and white mousseline bed curtains are all by Agnès Comar.

Right: A chaise longue by Christophe Pillet sits close to the bed, in front of a 1950s cabinet. The picture on the wall is by Suzanne Valadon.

Below: The romantic bathroom with an oval bath by Villeroy & Boch standing on a slate base.

and accentuating the effect by using long pieces of furniture. In the salon a long sofa is placed along the wall, and four 1950s armchairs by Vestergaard Jensen, covered in raw silk, are placed around a mosaic table from the same period. In the dining room two long tables sit end to end while well-placed mirrors add perspective and a sense of space.

An immaculately tidy study leads directly to the bathroom – obviously a nice buffer zone between work and relaxation – where a magnificent old-style bathtub is set on a heavy slate base. The bathroom is not at all tucked away but presented as a room with the same status as others, and leads onto the master bedroom. Here there is a strong Japanese atmosphere: the large bed is a mattress set on a base with a headboard on the wall. Agnès Comar is renowned for her exquisite bed and table linens and they are in evidence in the bathroom and bedroom, as elsewhere in the apartment. There are touches of fun as well – upstairs she has decorated a room for her grandsons in washed denim.

The restless designer, poised for fresh projects like an exotic, perpetually migrating bird, cannot say how long she will perch on the Left Bank, but it is unlikely to be for long. "One day perhaps I shall do a house to keep – I have it in mind – but not yet. I am too busy working and travelling for that."

LIFE IN THE COUNTRY
Le Bonheur est dans le Pré

France is an agricultural country, but most of the population lives in cities and towns. The majority of urban sophisticates have deep rural roots, however, and nourish dreams of getting back to them in old family homes, seaside cottages, stone sheepfolds or farms. They long to escape from city stress in order to paint, think or simply to replenish body and soul. This enchantment with the beauty, variety and relative emptiness of the French countryside draws people from all over the world.

MAS MIREIO

JACQUES GRANGE: PROVENCE

*Left: The old shepherd's
house, with its dusty pink
shutters, is a Provençal
dream. Jacques Grange
(below) feels that he was
lucky to have found it.*

Saint-Rémy sits at the epicentre of the Provençal myth, a closely
curled circular village of red-tiled roofs and narrow medieval streets,
belted by a wide boulevard lined with fat, leafy plane trees. Signposts
point outwards in enticing directions – Les Baux, Maussane,
Avignon, Cavaillon, Arles – reminding us that we are in the historic heartland
of Mistral, Daudet and Pagnol, of shepherds, vines and summer fruits, bulls
and waving pampas. The wide fertile plain of the Rhône delta bordered by
the rough grey rocks of the Alpilles is, in our collective imagination, above
all the landscape of Van Gogh.

The village has all the telltale marks of a tourist Mecca: gift shops selling
lavender soap, a local pottery and copies of *Les Lettres de mon Moulin*; cafés
with busy terraces thronged with a motley crowd of visitors. Saint-Rémy has
been called an inland Saint-Tropez. In the countryside around, grand new villas and modest old farm dwellings, renovated to glory undreamt of by their
original inhabitants, are among the most sought-after second homes in France.

Some say that Saint-Rémy has become insufferably smart, but on the whole it wears its chic
with insouciance. Nothing has fundamentally changed and you can still wander down a wind-
ing lane from the town and find a house that seems lost in time.

Such is that of Jacques Grange, one of France's most successful and innovative decorators, although "decorating" does
not really describe what he does. Grange is an inspired creator
of atmospheres, a *metteur en scène*, an architect of the interior
with an unrivalled sense of style and a great sense of humour.

"When I came to Saint-Rémy fifteen years ago I wasn't really
looking for a house; but when I saw this one I said straightaway,
'I'll take it.' It was a *coup de foudre*. I didn't realize it was special,
I thought everyone in Provence had a house like this. It was *très*
good luck for me to find it."

Jacques Grange believes that location is all important, and
the setting here is perfect. The property is on rising ground, part

*Above: The ceramic-topped
table is laid for lunch on the
shady terrace. Cane chairs,
simple pottery jugs and
plates, bowls of olives and
chunky coloured glasses
add to the relaxed Provençal
atmosphere.*

*Left: Jacques Grange, one
of France's most successful
and creative decorators,
relaxes on the terrace of his
Saint-Rémy home.*

Left: The low-ceilinged living room contains an eclectic mix of objects, pictures and furniture that the owner has collected on his travels.

Above: The piercing eyes of a fiesta bull from Bayonne seem to size up guests. Jacques Grange is fascinated by the culture of bullfighting.

Right: An old amphora by the door on the cobbled terrace.

Left: The typical Provençal farm kitchen fireplace, where all the shepherd's cooking would have been done, nowadays adds warmth and light to the room. On the shelf above sit fishermen's floats, a lobster pot and vegetable and egg baskets.

Right: The kitchen was kept as simple and authentic as possible, with open shelving for easy access. A pretty alabaster light fitting hangs over the table and chairs that are from the 1940s.

of the estate surrounding a chateau, overlooking the plain towards the Alpilles. The view from the edge of the garden Grange describes as "the view of Van Gogh". And so it is – a panorama of *garrigue* (scrubland) and cypresses, with the Alpilles in the distance.

Turning back you face the house, a stone-built L-shaped dwelling tucked shyly behind large garden trees; it is painted, shutters and all, a soft musty pink and is well clad in rampant greenery. "I kept the original colour; I have left the house much as it was, done as little as possible. I think of it as the Maison de Monsieur Séguin." (From the famous story by Alphonse Daudet written in nearby Fontvieille.)

Behind the house is the track taken by the celebrated shepherd, Bacullard, every year in the time-honoured journeys of transhumance. When Jacques Grange's friend Princess Caroline of Monaco lived next door she and her son joined the joyous procession. It was Grange who brought the Princess to Saint-Rémy after the death of her husband, Stefano Casiraghi. She too found it wonderfully peaceful, and when Jacques told her there was a house to rent she took it at once.

The *bergerie* (shepherd's house) is a very personal place for a man who spends his time imagining and creating houses, often very grand ones, for others: he has worked on Ronald Lauder's house at Palm Beach, USA and the home of Yves Saint Laurent and Pierre Bergé in Tangier, for example, and he is currently working with Lord Cholmondeley at Houghton Hall in England.

Jacques Grange's home is very different: "It is to please me, no one else," he says. "It is a place of happiness; I think of it as the house of *mon enfance conservé* (my childhood preserved). It is a great pleasure when I leave Paris to feel that I arrive in another country, because here we are already in Italy."

The house, where he spends about two months every summer and often comes in winter to relax, is full of objects, toys and memorabilia from places he has visited and events he has enjoyed. They are sometimes elegant, sometimes slightly crazy – like the huge thirteenth-century broadsword in its stand by the front door as if guarding the place.

His love of the rituals and traditions of bullfighting (important in the culture of the region) is evident throughout the house. In the salon a rack is hung with basket-weave heads of fiesta bulls; a large practice bull stands in the corner casting a bemused eye over the elegant but unfussy furniture. (Grange mixes epochs effortlessly: chairs by twentieth-century designers stand alongside a Louis XIII *fauteuil*.)

Above: The sitting room contains an interesting ensemble of twentieth-century furniture and a painting of a dinosaur. The hourglass table is typical of the curiosities that the owner loves to collect.

But Grange takes as much pleasure in a pair of gaudily painted candlesticks from a *brocante* market as he does in a highly valuable piece. The oddball amuses him, as in two remarkable small tables: one made from a tree-trunk beehive topped with a slate slab and resembling a giant mushroom, the other in the form of an enormous hourglass.

Easels and a large worktable are reminders that there is a creative aspect to life here, too. A library is crammed with books on art and design and local history. Bedrooms are calm and uncluttered – apart from pictures and posters and, in one, an enormous papier-mâché toreador by Mathias and Natalia.

Lunch is served on a ceramic table under a bamboo-covered pergola outside the kitchen door. The dappled sunlight illuminates the coloured glasses, the salad is fresh from the market and a sense of well-being spreads.

The garden is mainly lawn and trees, set with Adirondaks chairs and garden furniture from the 1950s. The pool is hidden discreetly behind a high hedge, with a dressing room that is another

Above: A lectern holds prints and books while strings of Easter eggs dangle below, beside a row of sunglasses.

Right: The library is over-flowing with books on art, design and local history. Pictures are propped against the shelves.

Below: A guest bedroom has a tree-stump beehive with stone slab on top as a bedside table.

Left and right: Jacques Grange has had fun decorating and furnishing the interior of this Romany caravan with lace and satin in authentic gypsy style.

Below: The brightly coloured gypsy caravan from the Camargue that is used as a resting place and changing-room for the swimming pool.

Grange surprise: a perfectly restored and furnished gypsy caravan from the Camargue peeks from behind the trees, a little like a gaudy railway carriage. Children can rest here in the afternoon; otherwise it is simply another marvellous plaything in a house of games.

The *bergerie* is his and not his; Grange rents it from the chateau's owners. "Why own? I think houses should be lightweight, they should not weigh you down. I like small houses, not palaces."

This lover and creator of "atmospheres" for years rented perhaps the most atmospheric apartment in Paris, that in the Palais Royal where the novelist Colette lived. It still belonged to her estate, but recently he was able to buy it, the family having said it was clearly meant for him.

Ownership, however, is not important to Grange; it is occupation and use that matter. Even when he is not here the thought of the *bergerie* sustains him. "It is my equilibrium. I can breathe here, I need to know it exists."

He was amused by the title of this book, which can suggest looking at life through rose-tinted spectacles. "*La Vie en Rose?* That's good, yes it works in the sense of a good life, a happy one."

128

LA FERME BLANCHE

PIERRE PASSEBON: TOURAINE

Left: The garden was designed by Louis Benech. The fairy-tale atmosphere is enhanced by stone "mushrooms" of a kind often used to prop grain stores off the ground, out of the reach of rats.

Right: The restored barn that the owner has transformed into a stylish and comfortable home for weekends.

The valley of the Loire is France's Valley of the Kings, a lush green landscape thronged with an improbable number of glorious castles and fortresses, mainly from the medieval and Renaissance periods. Here, on the banks of the country's majestic river and its tributaries, monarchs and their friends built extravagant palaces to which they could retreat to contemplate, hunt or simply live in glory. The patron whose spirit still hovers over this region of Touraine is that of the great sixteenth-century Valois king François I, who spent most of his reign building the palace at Chambord and consulting with his illustrious guest from Italy – Leonardo da Vinci, whom he installed at Amboise.

Given this ambience, converting a humble barn seems almost like cheek and there is certainly a youthful, witty atmosphere in Pierre Passebon's country retreat. He devised it in response to his sister's wish to somehow hold on to the family home near Amboise where they had grown up. This is a beautiful sixteenth-century mansion, a product of the Renaissance flowering, which their mother had decided to sell as it had become too difficult to manage on her own. In a happy compromise, Pierre agreed to take on one of the stone outbuildings and renovate it for his own use, and so the sale was cancelled.

In Paris, Pierre Passebon runs his own gallery dedicated to the decorative and applied arts and specializing in twentieth-century furniture. It is situated in the delightful Galerie Véro-Dodat, one of the city's pretty arcades that in recent years have seen a renaissance of their own; the little shops, once rather dilapidated, now sparkle with antiques, pictures, fabrics and gastronomic delicacies.

At weekends, however, Pierre likes to get away from the city, and thanks to the TGV (high-speed train) he can be in Touraine within an hour. The best thing about his home there, he says, is the garden, designed by Louis Benech, the famous landscape and garden designer who restored part of the Tuileries Gardens in Paris, among many other projects. To enjoy maximum benefit

Above: An ornate oil-lamp from the south of France hangs over the table in the kitchen and dining room. The two high-backed chairs are of the English Arts and Crafts movement; the other chairs are by Charlotte Perriand, who was a pupil of Le Corbusier.

Left: The library corner with a neo-classical French (c. 1820) chair in the foreground. The doll once belonged to Marlene Dietrich, who used to keep several dotted around her Paris apartment. The triangular table is by Charlotte Perriand and the high-backed Troubadour chair behind is from England, c. 1860.

Right: The main living area with its cut limestone fireplace is surmounted by a panel of ceramic tiles from Damascus. The nearest chair is by Charlotte Perriand; the narrow-backed armchair is in American Mission style, and the low table on the left is by Paul Frankel. The mahogany column to the left of the fireplace is by Marcial Berro.

Left: The large photograph propped against the wall, left, is by François Marc Barnier; the sheep seats are by François Favier La Lanne. A telescope stands ready for star-gazing. The ceramic chair in the foreground is Swedish and dates from 1930, while the table is eighteenth-century, despite its very modern design.

Right: A painting by Pierre et Gilles hangs above a 1925 cabinet by Francis Jourdain. Religious figures of Mary and Joseph are in biscuit porcelain.

Below: A vase by Suzanne Ramier, from the Valauris workshop also used by Picasso. To the right of it is an opaline dish, c. 1900.

from his garden, Pierre created a very large window to open directly onto it and the country-side beyond. The land falls away quite steeply and gives the feeling that the house is floating.

Inside there is an atmosphere of relaxation, comfort and amusement. It is a far cry from the typical "country cottage"; this is the hideaway of an elegant Parisian who has brought a touch of his city world with him to a place where things can be taken less seriously. To begin with, says Pierre, there was nothing whatsoever in the barn; it was just a huge empty space. This made it possible for him to do whatever he wished, and he and his mother simply paced out the rooms, deciding impromptu to put a door here, a window there. The main room is focused on a large fireplace, made in local cut limestone and fashioned to look like a frame. The floors are either terra-cotta tiles or simple floorboards; walls have been plastered with sand and lime and left unpainted – Pierre likes the natural colour of the plaster and in any case wanted soft tones throughout most of the house to reflect the greys, blues and yellows prevalent in the region.

The interior of the house was designed in concert with Pierre's friend Jacques Grange. The furniture is an eclectic mix: there are chairs by twentieth-century designers such as Le Corbusier, pieces from earlier periods and items found on trips to Africa. There is one large sofa. Two large woolly sheep – for sitting on – look as if they had just wandered in from the fields outside. Bookcases line the wall facing the fire. The kitchen-cum-dining room is more "countrified" in atmosphere than the rest of the house with a long refectory table, a fireplace and built-in dressers and cupboards in a traditional style.

The walls of the main bedroom are covered in original designs from the great American comics of the 1950s and 60s – Superman, Tarzan and Flash Gordon. Collecting these is one of the owner's passions, and he never ceases to be amazed by the high quality of the draughtsmanship and the artistic quality of the work. Only in the spare bedroom, tucked high up under the apex of the roof, has he abandoned restrained colours and gone for bold modernity. Here the quilt is bright cerise pink silk with a yellow lining, the carpet is a multi-coloured abstract 1950s design, and two prints of Andy Warhol's famous Marilyn Monroe portrait are placed against a wall.

This is a house in which the owner enjoys the company of friends and which provides a setting for the large number of *objets*, artefacts and pieces of furniture that he loves to collect. At the outset the space was, Pierre says, almost too big. Now the rooms are overflowing with things that he loves.

Above: The guest bedroom under the eaves, with easy chair and stool. The bed and stool are by Jean Royau. The cabinet to the right of the window is a "fortune-teller" cabinet from an English fairground. In it are two cardboard sculptures by Matthias and Natalia.

Right: The bedside table is in loupe de bouleau *birchwood veneer, and once belonged to Chateaubriand. The table-lamp is by Antonioz, and the large painting above the bed is by Pierre Lesieur.*

136

LA MAISON VERTE

CHRISTOPHER HOPE AND INGRID HUDSON: MINERVOIS

Left: The enchanting terrace behind the house is shaded by a wisteria and rush matting laid on a cast iron pergola; the old café table and chairs came from a local junk shop and the modern half-moon bas-relief was a birthday present to Ingrid from Christopher.

Right: Christopher Hope and Ingrid Hudson at home. They both love trawling through antique shops and brocantes *looking for unusual objects.*

Where the Minervois vineyards sweep northwards from the Mediterranean plain to touch the slopes of the Montagne Noire just east of Carcassonne, the medieval village of Caunes nestles close around its splendid eighth-century abbey. In its narrow lanes Ingrid Hudson tends a mini-empire of ancient houses that she has saved from ruin and transformed into havens of peace and nostalgia.

One of these is home to Ingrid and her partner Christopher Hope, the writer and broadcaster; the others are rented or have been sold on, but with Ingrid still as manager-minder. Several are in the same street and were acquired by default – in France you often get more than you bargained for when you buy an ancient village ruin.

Ingrid and Christopher bought their house in the mid-1990s, for just a few thousand pounds, but were surprised to discover that unexpected extras were crumbling dwellings and barns that looked as if nothing would save them from imminent collapse (and in one case didn't). But the buyers were delighted with them: their village-within-a-village began.

House one has since been renovated and sold to a friend, the writer and former publisher Carmen Callil; Ingrid and Christopher have moved into a larger dwelling next door. Two other houses are complete, two more remain to do.

The couple came to Caunes serendipitously in the early 1990s; Christopher Hope is not quite sure why, but getting lost is a speciality of his and falling in love had something to do with it too. He has described the discovery of "his" village and new home in a black-comic satirical-lyrical book, *Signs of the Heart – Love and Death in the Languedoc.*

"My house had an earth-floor cellar, a crumbling terrace covered by a spreading vine, a squat toilet in the corner of the garden and a pomegranate tree. It sat astride the old village ramparts and looked across the vineyards towards Corbières and beyond them the Pyrénées. Below the ancient fortifying wall, falling sheer to the road some ten metres below was the open-air wash-house … across the road were the vegetable gardens and the river."

Left: The painted dressing
table looks old, but dates only
from the 1950s. The spoon-
backed chair and mirror are
copies found in an antique
market. Only the pretty wall
sconces are authentic.

Right: In the dining room
the rustic fireplace has been
enlivened by a frieze embroidered with bluebirds, which
stops the chimney smoking. A
Spanish chandelier overhangs
a traditional farm table; the
curtains are made from linen
sheets. A French family
portrait in the corner boasts
a sumptuous gilt frame.

Below: Lace curtains from
Camden Passage, London,
hang over an internal window.
A figurine stands proudly atop
a marble-topped washstand.

These days the terrace is on firm foundations and the vine properly tamed and productive; beds of long-stemmed flowers reach up from the little walled garden; a laden loquat tree spreads in the centre; and a riot of solanum drenches the walls. Swallows dip and soar around the abbey towers and the bells toll the hours "five minutes late, as they have always done", notes Christopher. In between, the town hall's loudspeakers bray and crackle to tell you who is dead and what kind of produce is for sale on the main square. A preoccupation with love and death perhaps – but also food. This is France, after all.

South African-born and a photographer as well as a decorator, Ingrid recalls how they started out with just two deckchairs and a stolen teaspoon. Since such humble beginnings she has slowly, but with great sureness and style, restored and rebuilt the assorted houses and acquired a treasure trove of furniture and pictures and *bibelots* to embellish them. So much so that on first entering

the houses you feel you have, Alice-like, walked through a looking-glass into a corner of old France. It is, of course, a latter-day reinvention, a romantic and more colourful illusion of what such a home might have been, plus the comforts of plumbing and electricity.

The houses are repositories for myriad *objets trouvés*. Ingrid and Christopher both love their perennial trawls through the local *brocante* warehouses and barns, especially on the Montagne Noire, the range of forested hills that rises steeply to the north behind Caunes. Christopher is haunted by the ghosts of the former owners of the discarded and dust-laden possessions that they find in these surreal emporia; the juxtaposition of the jumble he finds "strange and terrible".

They acquire more of it relentlessly – at the great monthly *déballage* (literally "unwrapping") at Béziers (on the first Sunday in the month) and Montpellier (four times a year) and by simply scavenging here and there in skips and dumps. There are also the ever-enlarging Sunday attic sales (*vides-greniers*) in the villages, with professional and amateur sellers and dealers vying with private citizens to sell everything from kitchen tools, linen sheets, family portraits and oil lamps.

Christopher Hope came here, not to junk-hunt, but seeking a quiet place in which to write. The business of buying and the din of renovation – falling masonry and drilling – quickly laid low that idea. Now, somewhere on the other side of the street, behind a rough-hewn façade and with little more than a *meurtrière* (arrow slit) for natural light, Christopher holes up by day, scratching out a first draft of his latest book.

It obviously worked, as he has completed four books here, including the one about the village and his recent much-praised novel, *Heaven Forbid*, which was based on his childhood in South Africa. At the time of writing he was finishing a book about tyrants – of the kind whose busts and portraits garnish the junk heaps.

Above: The chintz-covered sofa in the sitting room came from an antiques market. The picture above it was painted in the mid-1930s and idealizes the new paid holidays for workers.

Left: A wall was knocked down to ensure a good "flow" of movement from the dining room to the sitting room and through onto the terrace. Part of an old firescreen hangs on the left; the picture on the right is appliqué work from South Africa.

Above: Metal slatted shutters in the sitting room create a tropical atmosphere. The pretty cast iron console, c. 1930, is topped by an art nouveau mirror; an old kilim is spread before the twin velvet armchairs from the 1950s.

Meanwhile, Ingrid Hudson labours on in her houses and their tiny gardens, bringing light and colour into what were once poky, dark little dwellings. Walls have come down and windows added. For Ingrid, space is paramount. "I like spaces that follow well," she says. "As far as decoration is concerned, finding out what was here and learning the old techniques was most exciting."

Lime – *chaux* – is much used in plaster mixes and for paint effects. Pigments such as the green and blue lime-wash in the living room and the torrid pink of the terrace walls come from Daniel Faure, owner of the only live lime kiln in France, in the Montagne Noire near Castres. Monsieur Faure, a diminutive, bearded genius, was plainly enchanted by the elegant Ingrid in her straw hat and earrings. He even mixed a special colour for her called *"Bleue Ingrid"*, using eight different pigments. Stunningly beautiful in the pot, unfortunately by the next day the colour had vanished back into white. "One blue ate another," says Ingrid ruefully.

She collects embroidery typical of the region: the linen chimney cloth over her main fireplace is a frieze of delicate bluebirds winging across a Never-Never Land sky. She also looks for

Left: In the main bedroom the bed's silk brocade tasselled hangings were put together by Ingrid from "bits and pieces" she found. The long pillow on the bed is a genuine gypsy hand-embroidered cushion filled with straw.

Below: The spare bedroom is decorated with brass and cast-iron beds, white cotton covers and old quilts found in the cellar of the house. The walls are painted with blue lime-wash, and a screen on the left is decorated with postcards.

fragments of local textiles and *boutis*, the traditional close-quilting technique used for bed-covers and even skirts to pad out the trousseau chests. Cast-iron work also delights her and she has found local craftsmen to make railings, pergolas and garden staircases.

Although previously more modern, Ingrid's taste is now less serious and purist. She likes pretty things and admits that chandeliers are a minor obsession – "the sillier the better" – as well as old photographs and pictures of goodness-knows-who to add atmosphere, and more ghosts for Christopher to commune with.

A favourite and highly atmospheric acquisition is a large oil painting from about 1935 showing an idealized young family on the river bank: the father fishing, the mother breast-feeding her baby. "It is from the time of the first paid holidays in France, an idyllic image of a break in the countryside that was suddenly within the reach of ordinary city folk." says Ingrid.

They are foreigners in France, but have taken their chosen patch to their hearts and made it their own, interpreting it in a way that pleases even their French neighbours – who think all foreigners are slightly mad, but are nevertheless touched and pleased to see their neglected buildings restored and discarded heirlooms spruced up. The partnership is a good one both in imaginative and in practical terms: Christopher is ironic and shy with a savagely amused eye on his fellow man, while Ingrid, like a worker-bee, creates her cellular habitat around his secret centre.

LA TOUR HUGUES DE SABANAC

KEN HOM: LA VALLÉE DU LOT

Left: A metal garden table decked with cacti, an old lantern against a closed nail-studded door, ivy creeping up the stonework and a stone dog welcome visitors to La Tour Hugues de Sabanac.

The hinterland of Cahors, one of the great medieval cities of southwest France, is the country of *Le Prince Noir et le diamant noir* – the Black Prince and the black diamond – the fearsome English invader from the Hundred Years' War and the indigenous truffle, beloved of gourmets the world over.

The prince and his army are long gone, but the region remains celebrated for its truffles and wine and is also rich in game, poultry, *foie gras*, walnuts and all manner of delicious fresh produce. "The land of good living" they call it and it certainly inspires good cooking and hearty eating in a fertile, wooded landscape.

Ken Hom, one of the world's greatest Chinese cooks, came home to roost here more than a decade ago. He had fallen in love with the region following visits to his friends the Pebeyres, a well-known family of truffle negociants, and decided to look for a home. It had to be a village house (Ken does not drive) and have a garden, not always an easy combination to find in southern France. After a long search with his partner, Ken did the sensible thing and consulted another chef: Alexis Pelissou of Le Gindreau at Saint Médard reckoned he knew just the right house.

They set out for Catus, a small market town about eighteen kilometres from Cahors. Ken looked around and liked what he saw, remarking in particular on a stone building with a singu-

lar high square tower as being incredibly beautiful. "That's it," Pelissou said triumphantly, and so it was.

Ken loved the vast vaulted wine cellar at first sight; his partner was enchanted by the small indoor courtyard that confronts the visitor on entering the wide, round-arched front door. A deal was struck. The price at the time seemed cheap but renovation of the house was to prove quite an undertaking – to bring a medieval *barraque* back to life and warmth and to install the particular requirements of a cook who likes to entertain on a generous scale.

The house was built for a nobleman, Hugues de Sabanac; the foundations date back to 1285, but the tower was added later during the Hundred Years' War as a lookout against the English who did capture Catus, tower and all, three times. Even

Left and above: The medieval arches and stonework of the entrance hall and stairs to the house are festooned with greenery, giving a mysterious and romantic effect. The foundations of the house are from the thirteenth century.

now it is still known locally as "*la tour des Anglais*". Ken enjoys the irony that he came from England to acquire it and brings many English guests to visit, not least the British Prime Minister and his wife, Tony and Cherie Blair. They have become regular visitors, coming to dine during their annual summer holiday in the area. Ken has even hosted an informal mini-summit when the French Premier Jean-Pierre Raffarin joined the party. It is believed that the Black Prince himself stayed here once, but it is unlikely that he ate so well.

The house that Ken found was in a state of disarray and dereliction and had been empty for eight years. The previous owners had spent all their available money on the structure and the exterior (following the draconian demands of the French conservation authorities), but the inside was a disaster area: the tower, accessible only by ladder, was full of pigeon waste and the windows were without glass, so what little heat there was escaped upwards. The whole interior had to be rebuilt and recreated.

Some things were immutable: at street level the front door opens to an ancient stone-paved hall with a wide stone staircase leading upwards (another goes down to the wine cellar, now containing between 3,000 and 4,000 bottles). The little courtyard, beautifully planted, is closed off by glass in the interests of warmth.

On the first floor the main room of the house is, predictably, a huge kitchen. Three smaller rooms were broken down to make what is now a marvellous theatre of cuisine, dedicated to the pleasure of cooking and eating, for chef and diners alike. It is a long room, with south-facing French windows along one side opening to a garden, which comes as a pleasant surprise at this level. There is a large fireplace at one end of the room, overhung by a copy of a Dutch still life of a hare and game birds. ("I found it in a *brocante*," explains Ken. "It seemed suitable.") A *rotisserie* nestles in the grate space, and can be removed if wished to make an ordinary fire. But for the chef, nothing seems more agreeable than to watch your

Left: A close-up of the nameplate on Ken Hom's Maestro cooker, the model made for the world's top chefs.

Right: A view of the great kitchen-dining room, with the full batterie de cuisine and the monumental cooker. Ken likes to cook and talk to his guests at the same time.

duck roasting as you work up an appetite. Ken loves to descend on Tour Hugues de Sabanac impromptu with a group of friends and set to work, while they talk and argue, sampling the local wines and delicacies.

At the other end of the kitchen, ceiling-high cupboards contain plates and glasses and also serve to conceal the galley – a narrow washing-up area. A French refectory table, which can seat fourteen, runs down the centre of the room; a massive butcher's block is to the right of the door-way; and an early wooden refrigerator provides more cupboard space. But in the corner by the fireplace is the *pièce de resistance* – a magnificent Maestro cooker, the model that Bonnet Cidelcem makes for chefs around the world. This one was custom-made for Ken Hom, whose name is stamped on it in brass, with a small knife and fork on each side.

"It weighs several tons and cost the price of a good car," says Ken, who finds it a "joy and luxury" to cook in this kitchen. "I have plenty of space around me and I can entertain my friends at the same time." He frequently entertains other chefs. Of the local produce, truffles are his especial delight, and he has always loved *confit de canard*, as it reminds him of Chinese preserved duck, although in that recipe the bird is dried in salt rather than cooked in its own fat.

In winter, or for small groups of guests, the dining room across the hall is used. With its ornate panelling and elegant fireplace, it looks like a perfect eighteenth-century room, but it was just an empty space before renovation. They found the fireplace and built around it. Some of the panelling is old, and some copied. The effect is warm and comfortable.

"French craftsmen may take a long time but they do a good job," says Ken. He has special praise for the local *menuisier* (cabinet-maker), Thierry Florentin, who also created the intriguing library for 3,500 cookery books in the tower and made some beautiful shelves in the kitchen.

Left and Right: The dark oak panelling and a beautifully carved mantelpiece, commissioned by Ken Hom to cover the cold stone walls in his small sitting room and dining room, give a warm, intimate atmosphere. The fanciful modern lamp with coloured tulip-like shades was brought from Paris.

There were originally 7,000 cookbooks in the library, but Ken weeded them down. He does not use them to cook from, just as reference and for ideas and techniques.

Bedrooms are tucked under the eaves of the main house and are simple and comfortable with a touch of colour and refinement added by Oriental artefacts and figures. A Buddha occupies a niche in the oldest intact room in the house, to which no change was permitted.

The tower these days is approached by a new and impressive oak staircase and there are perfectly fitting shutters on the windows. Past the chef's library, another stair leads to the very

Left: An eighteenth-century sofa, upholstered in brocade, is positioned next to a medieval window seat. The shutters in the house were handmade to a close fit by a local craftsman.

Below: A closet painted in a traditional French style in one of the bedrooms.

Above: The main bedroom is a calm, simply furnished room, reflecting the main function of the house as a place of relaxation.

top floor, which is used by Ken's partner, a sculptor, as a studio. Many of his works are on display in the house, especially his remarkable tiny painted figures, some whimsical and witty, some decorative, many expressive of a range of emotions, like miniature mimes. He may well spot some invading *Anglais* from his high vantage point but they will probably only be here for the truffles and cheese on market day.

The finished house is a modern masterpiece within a solid medieval shell. "I have to live in big cities – Paris and London – so this house is to relax in and a place to put all the things we keep acquiring," says the owner. "I love the historic side of it, but we try not to live like pseudo-medievals; that would be nonsense."

LE JARDIN SECRET

LESLEIGH: LUBERON

Left: Antique white linen sheets were used to cover the cushions for the welded steel frame sofa that Lesleigh designed for the living room in her restored silkworm farm. Her large mask sculpture on the wall is called "Refracted Man" and is covered with tiny pieces of mirror. Circles of heavy glass have been placed on Burmese frog-drums as tables.

Right: Sculptor Lesleigh on the roof-terrace which she created to replace a collapsed roof. She comes to Provence to work and breathe.

Below: Stone steps lead down to the "Secret Garden" from which the house is named.

The Luberon hills, stretching from Aix eastwards across northern Provence to Forqualquier, are a favourite summer haunt for a wide range of upmarket incomers, from French government ministers to film stars and fashion designers, a stylish crowd drawn by the magnificent scenery and the pretty medieval *villages perchés* and old stone houses.

Anyone who has been there or has seen the film of Jean Giono's *Le Hussard sur le Toit* (The Horseman on the Roof), which is set in the region, will understand the appeal of the Luberon's beauty and peaceful grandeur and, of course, its climate, sunny but less hot and humid than on the plain or near the coast. Long before the area became fashionable, artists and writers had been coming here for generations: Giono and film director and playwright Marcel Pagnol celebrated the bucolic life; latterly Peter Mayle hugely increased its popular appeal – to some residents' dismay – in his book *A Year in Provence*, which brought in the coach parties from around the world.

Lesleigh Goldberg (she uses only her first name professionally) arrived by a long route from her native Colorado, via Paris and with many an exotic stopover between. She is a sculptor – an artist working in three dimensions – although she has been striving to refine what that means, using laminated photographic images and a range of unorthodox materials to compose her works. She came seeking more space in which to breathe and work – a contrast to the constrictions of the city – and a warmer climate, with better light.

She lives in a large house in a hamlet near the village of Roussillon, famous for the red pigment in its earth, which, according to legend, resulted from a dramatic medieval suicide. The lady of the village is said to have jumped off a cliff above the village when she found out that her jealous husband had murdered her troubadour lover, cut out his heart and cooked it *à la provençale* for her dinner. (Good cuisine, albeit at a less grisly level, is still one of the Luberon's attractions: there are many excellent restaurants in the region.)

The house that Lesleigh owns – a former silkworm farm – was the very first one that she looked at. It dates from 1768 and was a near-ruin, but she fell in love with it, and although she looked at many others afterwards, this was the one that stayed with her. So she bought it and embarked on the inevitable large-scale renovation program. But, unlike Peter Mayle and others, she has no

Left: The U-shaped house frames the courtyard-garden which is shaded by two fig trees in summer. Lesleigh designed the steel garden table, setting shells in sand under glass for the top. The simple cane chairs are from from Ikea.

Below: Solid double doors lead to the village street. An old church bell hangs in the small window frame above, tolled by visitors to attract attention.

horror stories to tell: she escaped the usual problems because French friends found her someone reliable to oversee the works. "The main part of the house was done in seven months with no glitches," she says with some satisfaction.

Structurally, the style is simple and follows the original layout of the house: the most dramatic change was to replace part of a collapsed roof with a terrace and a small pool – a *bain romain* – which caused quite a sensation among Lesleigh's neighbours. The house is built in a U-shape round an interior courtyard, a wonderfully cool place in summer, with Lesleigh's witty variation on a provençal fountain – a face made up of pebbles and branches – spurting into a stone basin in one corner. Inside, she has created a studio apartment on the ground floor and a three-bedroom, three-bathroom home for herself and her partner above. All the ceilings have exposed beams and Lesleigh has used undressed stone walls in conjunction with a slightly rough-textured sand and cement plaster in soft natural colours to enhance the rustic atmosphere. Reminders of the building's original use are holes in the bedroom walls where the poles to hang leaves for the silkworms were once suspended. Lesleigh installed a practical and warming double-face chimney with simple stone surround so that the fire is visible in the salon and the dining room.

Above: "Grotto man" is an amusing fountain-head in the courtyard. It was made by Lesleigh from cement, and then studded with pebbles and twigs to suggest a scarecrow face.

Right: The roof-terrace is Lesleigh's sun-trap. Her bold construction of a pool up there, with a "Shell Man" sculpture piping water into the basin, amazed her neighbours. The chaises longues were bought locally; the table and chairs are perforated steel, designed by the owner. A perennial awning on a steel frame is made from a perforated synthetic fabric that lets the rain through and resists the wind.

Left: The picture beside the door in the sitting room is one of Lesleigh's photographic works – a portrait in which the image has been torn and woven together again. The tall copper lamp is one of several in the house that she made.

Above: The ornate carved chairs inlaid with shell and bone on each side of the fireplace are from Egypt. The fire is double-faced, and also opens onto the dining room. There are removable glass panels on each side.

Right: Another of Lesleigh's signature lamps. This one has a plain shade garnished with decorative metal dragonflies.

The furniture – a successful melange of antique and modern – was in part imported from Lesleigh's former loft in SoHo, New York; other things she made here, including the attractive lamps forged from copper piping in the master bedroom and the sitting room. Lesleigh was worried that her imports from America would be a disaster in their new setting. "But in fact I think that the pieces from my past life look better here than they did in New York." Many of them show an Asian or eastern influence. Her exquisitely ornate dining table was inspired by a visit to Egypt and made by a craftswoman friend who specializes in delicate gold-leaf techniques, imposing layers and sanding them down and then adding more. A dramatic hand-painted four-panelled screen from India hangs behind the table.

Lesleigh works here and in Paris: the great advantage of the Luberon, she says, is that there is more space than in her Paris studio and also a good team of artisans – iron-workers and the like – are always on hand. As a sculptor and artist she is evolving all the time. When she was very small, as a child in Colorado, she drew constantly – on walls, floors, anywhere – and was always "making things". After training at the University of Pennsylvania and at Berkeley, where she obtained her

Above: The main bedroom with all-white linen and cotton covers. A Syrian wedding chest is at the foot of the bed. The bedside tables and lamps are by Lesleigh: the shades have tiny glass drops wired around them.

Right: A haunting mural called "White Ladies in the Sky" in the main bedroom is 2.7 metres by 1.85 metres. It is a collage of photographs printed on canvas. The table in front of it was designed by Lesleigh in perforated steel.

Master's degree in Sculpture, she launched her own fashion label in New York, before returning to art. In her sculpture she has moved away from conventional materials and now works almost exclusively with photographic and computerized images, a development which has surprised her. She has done many portraits – "in a sense all my work is figurative" – including one of her neighbour in Provence, the actor John Malkovich. Recently she completed a series based on the female deities depicted at Angkor Wat, the greatest of the sacred temples of Cambodia, which she calls "A Moment of Grace"; this spiritual, Eastern element runs through much of what she does, and it has found a happy coalescence with the light and peace of the Luberon.

Left: The spare bedroom has a series of panels made from photographs of tulips in the process of decay. Below them is a superb Thai wedding chair designed to sit on an elephant's back, covered in a modern striped linen. The ornate table in the foreground is Louis XIV.

Right: The octagonal painting of zebras was painted by Lesleigh's mother. The bed is covered in a mix of antique and modern quilts and cushions covered in kimono silk. The holes in the walls were for the poles on which mulberry leaves for silkworms were hung.

LES PRES D'EUGÉNIE

MICHEL AND CHRISTINE GUÉRARD: LANDES

Above: Christine and Michel Guérard, who between them lead the field in healthy cuisine and authentic French country décor.

Left: Breakfast time in a bedroom at the inn of the Ferme aux Grives (Thrush Farm) restaurant, one of the small hotels that have been designed and decorated by Christine Guérard with discreet, flawless taste. The fireplace is eighteenth-century marble.

Right: The façade of the Ferme aux Grives restaurant, the barn that has become Michel Guérard's proving ground for his country cuisine.

The thermal spas of France were once as much part of the smart social round as they were cure centres. Monarchs and generals, duchesses and courtesans, anyone who was anyone flocked to these resorts and their monumental hotels to see and be seen while taking the waters in the hope of curing anything from gout to consumption. In recent years, the spas have enjoyed a major revival and now, once again, leaders and pacesetters of society, including politicians, businesspeople, and stars of entertainment and fashion, head the rush to seek cures, albeit more discreetly.

The most seductive of these revived and reinvented establishments is without question at Eugénie-les-Bains, in the Landes, the forested farming area not far from the Atlantic coast. At Eugénie (named for Napoleon III's Empress, who visited a few times) Michel and Christine Guérard have created a dreamy environment where health, elegance, wonderful food and décor – the very best of things French – combine to soothe and refresh. The 16-hectare (40-acre) park, with its four hotels, two restaurants and thermal installations, is much more than a spa although it is renowned, and people come from far and wide on medical referral for rheumatic and obesity problems.

Michel Guérard, who invented *cuisine minceur* (literally, slimming cookery) in the 1970s, was the pioneer of a lighter, healthier gastronomy later known generally as *la nouvelle cuisine*. He was inspired to do this when he saw how dull the food at the spa was. Nowadays at Eugénie, the cornucopia of his three-star restaurant in the main building runs in parallel with his *minceur* menus served at La Maison Rose, a hotel designed for residents taking the cure. The régime has become a little less rigorous: sugar and fat are still out, but a few cereals and vegetables are admitted.

Allied to Michel's gastronomic genius is that of his wife, Christine, who created and is continually developing the magical setting, the *cadre*, by which guests are embraced when they drive through the gates. The hotels (all within walking distance of each other) are paragons of comfort and excellence, of course. But while the main old spa hotel, parts of which date back to the first Napoleon, is superb in a traditional grand hotel manner, the three others are quite different. In restoring and decorating an old convent school, a solid farmhouse and a former notary's house as guesthouses, Christine Guérard not only played to the fantasies of her guests, but established herself as a leader of the revival of French country style in décor, translating French ideas of *luxe* into a new idiom of rural refinement.

Her achievement is the more astonishing since she was not artistically trained but had the intellectual education of a French high-achiever. Her career began in banking and she is now president of the group of twenty-two thermal establishments built up by her late, adored father, Adrien Barthélémy. Since he had no sons, Christine recalls, he wanted a businessman for a daughter. So, to please him, she became "the only boy in the family". Running a nationwide empire that treats 30,000 clients a year is hard and often exhausting work. But at Les Prés de Eugénie, she works hard all over again, allowing her creative side to blossom and, in collaboration with her husband, to bring what she calls their "secret garden" to perfection. And they do collaborate; there is no barrier between his domain and hers: she tastes his new dishes first; he gives his approval to her ideas for a new room.

Christine Guérard has been called an Amazon and she presides over her creation like a high priestess, with a formidable attention to detail and an unshakeable dedication to perfect standards. Her personal style is a mix of influences, perhaps from time spent in Mexico and Asia – her dark hair hangs free, she wears no makeup and likes to wear loose gowns and robes. Her decorative ideas are simple; indeed, she adheres to the paradox that luxury is simplicity.

Christine has an inborn genius for mixing comfort with country décor; her sympathy for old materials and natural fabrics and her love of pictures and objects collected in flea markets or at auctions combine to save her establishments from seeming overdressed and contrived on the one hand or institutionally bland on the other. Eugénie may be a kind of fantasy world, but at the same time everything here has solidity, a reality and a generosity of soul that come from its creator.

Christine approaches a decoration project by "listening to the house". She advises that anyone

who buys a property should also buy a sleeping bag and spend a night or two there before starting work on it – to find out how the light comes in, and to see it in different seasons if possible. Her small hotels bear witness to the value of this cautious, receptive approach.

Left: The door to the Ferme aux Grives restaurant in natural pine.

Right: The "Salon des Demoiselles" in the Inn at the Ferme aux Grives. The Louis XVI chairs are covered in fabric by Pierre Frey. In the eighteenth-century glass-fronted cupboards is an assortment of antique crockery collected by Christine Guérard.

Left: In the bedroom called "Joli Matin" the bed is "Grand Siècle" by Sempey and is covered in Pierre Frey fabric. The daybed is 1830s and also covered in Pierre Frey fabric. Chinese bedside tables are in pale mahogany; the lamps with rabbits are from Lieux. The Victorian armchair is covered in chic white cotton.

Right: A bathroom in the Inn at the Ferme aux Grives has a polished grey marble bath and shower-back. The ecclesiastical chair is nineteenth century.

The most recent of the hotels is the Ferme aux Grives (Thrush Farm), which was once a farm of that name. The old barn is now Michel Guérard's rustic restaurant, where he has developed a menu based on old-fashioned *cuisine grand-mère* – the stews and hearty fare of the country – adapted to *minceur* principles. The farmhouse behind is now a country inn of rare beauty – terra-cotta tiles, lime-washed beams and pale French grey paintwork set the rural tone. The salon's Louis XVI and early nineteenth-century furniture, covered in broad sunny yellow striped fabric by Pierre Frey, adds a touch of refinement. The *campagnard*, or rustic, atmosphere is reinforced at breakfast, served in the *chocolaterie*, where cupboards are filled with the farm's produce of jams and jellies alongside crisp white and yellow linen. The four extremely spacious bedrooms have romantic, curtained beds with eiderdowns and plump pillows. Log fires are lit in winter to increase the sense of being at home. Outside, a superb *potager* – vegetable garden – has been planted both as decoration and to provide wonderful things for the kitchen.

On the other side of the grounds is Le Couvent aux Herbes, a place Christine Guérard sees as a retreat, where busy or tired people can find peace and replenishment. The loveliest room is called Le Temps des Cerises (the time of cherries, or just "good times") on the ground floor, opening onto the garden. Jacques Chirac has stayed here, as have many other famous guests.

The *pièce de résistance* among the restored buildings is the Ferme Thermale, the leisure spa (as opposed to the medical establishment) available to hotel guests. This is a recreated Landaise half-timbered farmhouse, brought from the countryside and reassembled and adapted to its new purpose. In the entrance hall, a huge and voluptuous bust of the Empress Eugénie greets new arrivals; inside they will find some of Christine Guérard's most interesting conceptions – a carved marble table with a Roman grandeur where "patients" lie for a mineral water cure, chestnut wood barrow-beds with thick wool mattresses for resting on after treatments, and a marble bath filled with spring water and curative plants to soak in as a fire crackles in the salon's fireplace.

As the inventor of this paradise says, "luxury is simplicity".

Above: A detail of the exterior of the Ferme Thermale, an old Landaise farmhouse that has been reconstructed and transformed into a leisure spa where guests can have water treatments.

Left: At the Couvent des Herbes, this room is called "Le Temps des Cerises"; the name is underscored by Manuel Canovas' Tremolat fabric in giant pink and cream checks on the Louis XVI chairs. The bed hangings are in Natecru by Pierre Frey.

Right: An elegant salon comes as a surprise at the far end of the Ferme Thermale. Here a fire burns in the marble fireplace in winter and a fan cools the air in summer. The marble bath with swan taps was designed by Christine Guérard and made by Jean-Paul Bousquet.

LA ROCHE

GILLES SACKSICK: QUERCY

Right: Gilles and Isabelle Sacksick on the terrace of their house, in and around which the artist finds his greatest inspiration.

Left: The cavernous fireplace is surmounted by a fresco of everyday household objects. It was originally painted to conceal a soot stain.

The ancient fiefdom of Quercy, in the heart of the southwest, is quintessential rural France. Roughly, it is the modern *département* of the Lot, edged with slices of the Corrèze and Dordogne. A wealthy centre of commerce and agriculture since Roman times (as the grandeur of the capital, Cahors, indicates), it passed through periods of torment during the Hundred Years' War and the 1789 Revolution; these days it is a serene country of farms and villages, churches and chateaux. Here we are a long way from coastal temperament and garish colours, and safely down from brooding mountain closeness. This is *la douce France*, a landscape of rounded limestone hills and plunging valleys, of steeply pitched shingle roofs, worn like fantastic high hats on their walls of pale cut stone.

The house of artist Gilles Sacksick is in a small hamlet called La Roche, near Souillac. He lives there, but the house also lives in his head and in his heart, and in his work he paints and repaints its rooms, contents and surroundings in dreamlike sequences and a gently voluptuous style.

Access to the property is via a narrow gap between the house and adjacent barn (only manoeuvrable from one direction, drivers are warned). A short flight of stone steps leads to a terrace; a vine, heavy with ripe grapes in autumn, festoons the pergola over a door leading directly into the living room.

Gilles, who exhibits regularly both in France and around the world and was preparing for his seventh Paris show, opens the door to his tiny house – and thus on his work – with a natural, hospitable kindness.

Inside are heavy beams, a rich smoky smell, sunbeams striking along the broad floorboards and logs crackling on the fire; books and magazines are strewn on the table, a piano waits in the corner. Fruit, pot-bellied jugs, a *cafetière*, boots and shoes, a sleeping cat. All commonplace items at home, only here they are in duplicate – the tangible and the distilled artistic image. Which is more real? For Gilles, the old philosophical conundrum about the nature of reality is daily bread as he paints both what he sees and what he thinks.

Right: The gentle landscape of Quercy is a perennial element in artist Gilles Sacksick's subject matter.

Over the fireplace there is a fresco of jugs and kitchen utensils (where a soot stain used to be) and, around the room, suddenly a wonderful joke – a frieze of tiny grotesque heads, including one of a braying ass. "I like to think of him as me," says Gilles, smiling. A bit of fun is essential: "This is a monastery where the religion is laughter," he says of his somewhat austere workshop in the barn next door where his prints and woodcuts are made.

In the main house there are only four rooms – living room, kitchen, bedroom and, the largest, Gilles' studio with windows on three sides. "I can look at that landscape forever and never tire of it. It changes all the time. " This view (including the window frame) appears in many paintings. The change from the "brown sea" of fields in winter to the green luxuriance of spring is always the greatest miracle.

The floorspace is empty apart from an easel holding the canvas that is currently being worked on. There is a stool, and (an exotic touch) his fetish object, a much depicted brocade velvet nineteenth-century chair. It is placed in a corner as if ready for another model, or none.

Above: Weathered stone steps lead to the terrace in front of the house, which is sheltered from the sun by a prolific vine in summer.

174

Above: A plant in its pot at the bottom of the steps to the house. The garden is dotted with fruit trees and has a cabbage patch.

Right: La Roche is typical of houses in Quercy with its steeply-pitched shingle roof worn like a fantastical high hat on its walls of pale cut stone.

Paintbrushes are ranged with symmetry in jars on the mantel, while a large black umbrella is incongruously placed behind the ancient wood stove.

Gilles says the house is both the subject for his painting and the *atelier*, although he feels that it does not have to be this house – he would paint any house where he happened to live and it would be the same. He is emphatically not engaged in some *recherche du temps perdu*, or in love with old stones for their own sake. "I am not hooked on the past, not at all nostalgic," he says. "I live in the present."

Gilles and his wife Isabelle (a *brocanteuse* dealing in old textiles and linens) are people of uncommon warmth and openness. They have been married for nearly forty years and form an unusually close couple. "We are the freaks," he notes, smiling. "Everyone else has split up."

Gilles Sacksick's unusual name has a Balkan origin, he says, and his mother's family was Breton (a combination that perhaps accounts for his luminous brown eyes and thick dark hair). But he and Isabelle are true Parisians, intellectuals with the characteristic intensity and love of convivial, analytical talk typical of that milieu. His literary mentor, champion and great friend was the writer André Dhôtel; Robert Doisneau, the celebrated photographer, was also a great friend and took his last pictures here at La Roche. Dhôtel died in 1991, Doisneau in 1994. They are much missed.

Among the many critiques of Sacksick's work made by Dhôtel he left a touching epilogue: "I have made up my mind. You are not a painter who creates pictures, but an artist who is passionate about different lights … which never cease to enchant me."

Left: The artist's studio with brushes and pots ranged on the fireplace and an incongruous umbrella by the wood-burning stove.

Above: The front door that leads directly to the main living room. Paint-spattered shoes have been left by the threshold.

Right: A view from the studio towards the living room. The copper palate hanging on the wall is used for mixing colour with hot wax.

While Gilles' artistic influences are obvious – Chardin, Courbet, Vermeer, Rembrandt – there is, unsurprisingly, a literary, intellectual element in his approach. But it is unlikely that he could have painted as he has living all the time in Paris. Quercy and the house at La Roche have been necessary to him.

And, in the end, painting and drawing are what are important: "All the beauty of the world can be expressed with a school pencil and a scrap of paper." That beauty, for him, can best be found in his own house, his immediate family and in the countryside.

It was in the 1970s that Dhôtel urged him to "come and see the most beautiful countryside in the world". Gilles and Isabelle came, saw and bought a barn that was, in his words, little more than a heap of stones, and what they term their great adventure began. This is their country of adoption: their children grew up here, and in 1989 they moved a few miles to La Roche where they now spend stretches of time, returning to Paris to recharge and to exhibit and sell his work.

When he contemplates a new subject, "I look and look, and forget where I am. I think and think, and then at last it is all in my head. This takes a long time." Then, when he begins to paint it changes. "Then I think nothing at all. I work very quickly – a large painting takes only a few hours." He shrugs. "Who can tell where a painting begins, the exact moment? It is like trying to determine when love begins."

Left: A window and stool in the artist's studio, which are often depicted in his work.

Above: A still life composition.

Right: The studio with work in progress on the huge easel. "I look and look and forget where I am. Then I paint and work very quickly."

ANCIEN MONASTERE

CHRISTIAN LIAIGRE: ILE DE RE

Left: The living room, like the rest of the house, has walls lined with white-washed pine boards. Sofas are covered in white linen, and the stool is in stained beech. The fireplace is eighteenth-century and the red-orange tones of a kilim add colour to the décor.

Right: The harbour at nearby Saint-Martin, with yachts at anchor. Once only hardy Atlantic fishermen came to the island to unload their catches.

Above: The house was part of a monastery and, unusually for the Ile de Ré, has a large courtyard garden, now paved and embellished with pots.

The Ile de Ré is a narrow, curling slick of an island reaching out to the Atlantic just beyond La Rochelle. It is now linked to the mainland by a spectacular three-kilometre modern bridge, but its island identity remains. The Romans built a temple to Neptune here, Cistercian monks a monastery; in later centuries the island was a defensive outpost against sea-invaders such as the English, and a last resort for Protestants, pursued from within during the Wars of Religion. By the twentieth century the island had declined in population and prosperity to be the lonely preserve of fishermen and flocks of migrating birds, its flat salt-beds mirroring the empty sky.

About ten years ago, however, the Ile de Ré began to be "discovered" and quickly became one of the most fashionable resorts for Parisians and others seeking peace, pure air and pretty houses. It has something of the same status and atmosphere as the New England islands, a few thousand miles west across the ocean.

The designer and decorator Christian Liaigre is the high priest of French minimalism and can claim, more than most, that the island is his outpost; its light and "basic" qualities are an important and integral influence in his work. He was born in the Vendée (the ancient province in which Ile de Ré falls) and used to come over here, long before there was a bridge, to trundle around in a 2CV when there was little other traffic except bicycles and carts.

W magazine famously called Liaigre the "understated Zen master" of French interior design, a label that has stuck. He doesn't mind if he can translate it as synonymous with being a creator of peace – he believes that decorators should not aim to startle and amaze but to calm and soothe.

There are certain almost holy givens in his work and living: one such is the solid, hospitable table at the centre of things, recalling the monastic and farming life. The table is also highly relevant to

Left: A street of typical fishermen's houses in the village of Loix-en-Ré, where Christian Liaigre lives. The simple style of these dwellings is in tune with his own ideas.

Below: The front door, framed with the original stone, has been designed by Christian Liaigre in an austere, almost Japanese, style: squares of pine are laid on an interior layer of vertical planks.

Above: Panels of thick woven rushes from the local marshes are used as blinds in a summer garden room. They swing open to admit the light and air, or can be closed against too much sun or wind.

modern lifestyles in which the dining room has disappeared, or is used a few times a year and otherwise shut up like a museum exhibit.

In Christian's island retreat, which is, aptly enough, the remains of a monastery, the long refectory table is in wenge, a dark African wood, with stools made of chestnut. The atmosphere of the house is spare and calm, with bare floorboards, painted wooden walls and the staircase stripped back to the wood. Colours are beige and white, brown and black, relieved by a few measured touches of brightness, notably the pale red interior porch, painted in the colour favoured by local fishermen for their boats. The porch provides shelter from sea winds and a place to put bikes and sou'westers. This coral colour is echoed elsewhere in the house, as in a kilim on the

Left: The kitchen, like much of the house's design, has a nautical feel. The table, which Christian calls "Long Courrier" (long distance), is almost as long as the room and is made in wenge, his favourite wood from Africa. The chestnut stools around it were made in collaboration with Lou Fagotou. The work-surfaces are in teak and the cupboard doors are pine, stained with tar like the local fishing boats. Lights are by Conran.

Right: The window panes echo the design of the vestibule. A collection of seashells, found locally, sits next to coils of rope and canvas from Christian Liaigre's boat, a perfectly restored dinghy.

sitting room floor. Fabrics are used sparingly, and are mostly plain linen in natural shades or dyed dark grey-brown. Upstairs, a large master bedroom has a four-poster of gracefully simple lines, a desk and a camp bed; the teak-fitted bathroom has a shipboard feel. In one of the two guest rooms a Chinese lacquer bed seems positively exuberant, as do the Moroccan straw headboards and chairs in the other.

Embellishment is hyper-minimalist – navigational maps and oars on the walls, white coral in pots like frozen bridal bouquets, a stuffed, rather cross-looking, seabird. It is as if the house has been purged of all frippery, and indeed Liaigre has repeatedly expressed his dislike of *objets* and what he calls "decorative bulimia". "I am not an accumulator," he says. Clients, attracted by his thinking, often come to him asking what they can do to "get rid of all the furniture" they have collected or inherited. Some people believe that making empty space will change their lives,

Above: The "Opium" sofa by Christian Liaigre is in stained oak with grey-brown cushions. Armchairs are in stained beech. The leather screen from Cordoba is eighteenth-century.

Left: The delicate stucco-work of the mantelpiece is complemented by white coral brought back from Bora Bora.

Right: A glazed vestibule was designed as a protection against the Atlantic winds, and to stop sand getting into the house. When Liaigre was asked what colour he wanted it painted he said "crack open a crab and look at the inside of the shell." The red is also the colour used on fishing boats.

he says. But for him it is the light in the space that is most important: the island is very narrow – as little as 60 metres in some places – and thus the sea's reflection is everywhere.

Since acquiring this modest house in the 1990s, Liaigre has undertaken enormous and glamorous projects around the world, including a great gilded Paris mansion and a headquarters for Valentino, a New York apartment for Calvin Klein, a house for actress Carole Bouquet and assorted other houses from the Pacific islands to the Bavarian mountains. The Hôtel d'Alembert in Paris remains one of his great triumphs, as does the ultramodern Hotel Mercer in New York.

But all the while, his house, on one of the last patches of European land before the ocean and America, is there, virtually unchanging, like a tiny lighthouse, a touchstone of his style and philosophy. Not that he is at all high-minded or pompous about it. The spare background allows his friends to inhabit and complement it with gaiety and colour, he says; a bag of groceries, a discarded sweater, food on the table, all bring the house to life and show it "in its true nature".

Above: One bathroom is shared between three bedrooms: "If people come expecting luxury they have come to the wrong place," the host says. "This is a holiday house."

Left: The four-poster in the main bedroom is in wenge and shows a Shaker influence. The rug is North African, and the full-length curtains are in fine translucent cotton.

Right: The original staircase was stripped, but some traces of old paint remain. Wide floorboards are in raw oak. On the kitchen walls, seen behind, framed navigational maps are of other islands that Christian Liaigre has visited.

VISITOR'S GUIDE

THE DUCHE d'UZES
Open to the public every day except
Christmas Day.
Guided tours (approx 1 hour): July to mid-
September from 10h–13h and 14h–18h30,
Mid-September to end June from 10h–12h
and 14h–18h
Certain rooms and the gardens can be hired:
Le Duché d'Uzès
30700 Uzès, France
Tel: +33 (0) 466221896
Website: www.duche-uzes.fr

CHATEAU de COURANCES
Gardens and part of the chateau are open
Saturdays and Sundays from Easter to All
Saints (1 November) 14h–18h or by
appointment:
Chateau de Courances
91490 Courances, France
(50 kms south of Paris))
Tel: +33 (0) 164984118
Fax: +33 (0) 141050489
Email: courances@chateauxcountry.com

PHILIP HAWKES
Philip and Patricia Hawkes specialize in
selling chateaux and elegant apartments in
Paris:
6, rue Montalivet
75008 Paris

Tel: +33 (0) 142681111
Fax: +33 (0) 147422226

SEIGNEURIE de PEYRAT
To buy wine from the Seigneurie de Peyrat:
Tel: + 33 (0) 467249472
Fax: +33 (0) 467249352
Email: Seigneurie.de.Peyrat@wanadoo.fr

MEHMET and DIMONAH IKSEL
For more information about the Iksels'
decorative panels contact:
Iksel Decorative Arts (IDA)
Paris: +33 (0) 142965197
New York: +01 (212) 971 9736
Website: www.iksel.com

AGNES COMAR
For more information on Agnès Comar
design and products:
7 Avenue George V
75008 Paris
Tel: +33 (0) 147233385
Fax: +33 (0) 149520167

JACQUES GRANGE
Decoration et l'Architecture d'Interieur
118 rue du Faubourg Saint Honoré
75008 Paris
Tel: +33 (0) 147424734
Fax: +33 (0) 142662417

PIERRE PASSEBON
Decorative arts and twentieth century
furniture:
Galerie du Passage
20 Galerie Vero-Dodat
75001 Paris
Tel: +33 (0) 142 360113
+33 (0) 142366884
Fax: + 33 (0) 140419886

LA MAISON VERTE
To rent one of Ingrid Hudson's houses in
Caunes-Minervois:
Tel:+33 (0) 68784222
Email: IngridHudson@aol.com

CHRISTIAN LIAIGRE
Furniture and design showroom:
61 rue de Varenne
75007 Paris
Tel: +33 (0) 147537876
Email: sales@christian.liaigre.fr

LES PRES D'EUGENIE
Full details of hotel accommodation, cures
and special programmes:
Les Prés d'Eugénie
40320 Eugénie-les-Bains, France
Tel +33 (0) 558050505
Email: guerard@relaischateaux.fr
Website: www.michelguerard.com

BIBLIOGRAPHY

The French Chateau by Christiane de Nicolay-Mazery, Preface by
Philippine de Ganay, Thames & Hudson
The Most Beautiful Villages of France by Michael Jacobs,
Thames & Hudson
Indigo (history of the blue dye) by Jenny Balfour-Paul, British
Museum Press

The Seven Ages of Paris by Alistair Horne, Knopf
Languedoc Roussillon – Wines and Winemakers by Paul Strang,
Mitchell Beazley
Love from Nancy and *Letters of Evelyn Waugh & Nancy Mitford*
edited by Charlotte Mosley, Hodder & Stoughton

INDEX

Adami, Camilla 76
Adami, Valerio 74–81
Adenauer, Konrad 105
American Mission 132
Ancien Monastère 172–9
Angelico, Fra 87
apartments 64–81, 100–19
Apollinaire, Guillaume 75
Arts and Crafts 132
Aulenti, Gae 67

Bacou, Liliane 49
Bacullard 122
Bagès 109
Barnier, François Marc 135
Barthélémy, Adrien 166
Bauhaus 76, 79, 80
Belleville 90–9
Benech, Louis 131
Bennison, Geoffrey 54
Bergé, Pierre 126
Berlioz, Hector 75
Berro, Marcial 132
Black Prince 147, 148
Blair, Cherie 148
Blair, Tony 148
Bonnet Cidelcem 151
Bouquet, Carole 188
Bousquet, Jean-Paul 170
Braque, Georges 75
Buñuel, Luis 75
Burgundy 8, 28–37

Callil, Carmen 139
Canovas, Manuel 170
Caroline, Princess 122
Casiraghi, Stefano 122
Catus 8, 9, 147
Chardin, Jean-Baptiste 178
Chequers 53
Churchill, Winston 53
Clinch, Tim 8
Le Coeur, Jules 24
Colefax & Fowler 54, 73

Colette 128
Comar, Agnès 108–19
Comar, Anne-Cécile 109
Compain 92
Conran, Terence 185
Le Corbusier 76, 80, 83, 132, 136
de Courances, Château 7, 20–7
Courbet, Gustave 178
Le Couvent aux Herbes 170
de Crussol, Alessandra 16
de Crussol, Charles 16
de Crussol, Jacques 12–19

Daladier 16
Dali, Salvador 75, 76
Daudet, Alphonse 121, 124
Dégas, Edgar 75
Desmoulins, Camille 101
Dhôtel, André 175, 178
Dietrich, Marlene 132
Doisneau, Robert 175
Drian 66, 67
Dufy, Raoul 81
Dumas, Alexandre fils 75
Dürer, Albrecht 87

Eugénie, Les Prés d' 8, 164–71

Fagotou, Lou 185
de Fajac-la-Relenque, Château 56–63
Farrow & Ball 54
Faubourg-Saint-Germain 64–73
Faure, Daniel 143
Fayet, Gustav 53
Ferme aux Grives 165, 166, 169
La Ferme Blanche 130–7
Ferme Thermale 170
Florentin, Thierry 151
Fontfroide Abbey 53, 55
Foucault, Jean 75
Fragonard, Jean 75
François I 131
Frankel, Paul 132

Frey, Pierre 54, 166, 169, 170
Fujita 25

Gagnaire, Olivier 109
Galerie Véro-Dodat 131
de Ganay, Berthe 24, 25
de Ganay, Hubert 24
de Ganay, Jean-Louis 22, 24, 26
de Ganay, Philippine 7, 20–7
Gardillou, Didier 55
Garnier, Charles 101
Gascony 38–47
Gastou, Yves 111
de Gaulle, Charles 16
Gautier, Théophile 75
Giacometti, Alberto 81
Giono, Jean 155
Grange, Jacques 8, 109, 120–9, 136
Guérard, Christine 8, 164–71
Guérard, Michel 8, 164–71

Haussmann 90
Hawkes, Lucy 36
Hawkes, Patricia 8, 28–37
Hawkes, Philip 8, 28–37
Higgins, Bob 38–47
Higgins, Isabelle 38–47
Hom, Ken 8, 9, 146–53
Hope, Christopher 138–45
Hôtel d'Alembert 188
Hotel Mercer 188
Houghton Hall 126
Hudson, Ingrid 8

Iksel, Dimonah 100–7
Iksel, Kublai 101
Iksel, Mehmet 100–7
Iksel, Sinbad 101
Ile de France 20–7
Ile de Ré 172–9

Jansen 111
Le Jardin Secret 154–63

Jensen, Vestergaard 116
Joan of Arc 29
Jourdain, Francis 135

Klein, Calvin 188
Kokoschka, Oskar 80
Koulbak, Victor 82–9

Landes 8, 164–71
Languedoc 8, 48–55
La Lanne, François Favier 135
Lauder, Ronald 126
Lauragais 56–63
Leroy, Geneviève 56–63
Lesieur, Pierre 136
Lesleigh 154–63
Liaigre, Christian 172–9
lofts 90–9
Loix-en-Ré 182
Lot, Vallée du 146–53

Mackintosh, Charles Rennie 74, 75, 76, 81
McLenaghan, Michael 33
Mahloudji, Alidad 54
de Mail, Château 38–47
La Maison Rose 165
La Maison Verte 138–45
Malkovich, John 163
Malraux, André 16
Mann 70
la Marquise Rouge 15–16
Mas Mireio 120–9
Matta 79, 81
Matthias & Natalia 126, 136
Mayle, Peter 155
Michelangelo 85, 87
Minervois 138–45
Miró, Joan 81
de Missery, Château 8, 28–37
Mistral, Frédéric 121
Mitford, Nancy 66, 67, 70–3
Monroe, Marilyn 136
Montgomery, Bernard Law 22

INDEX

Montmartre 74–81

Montparnasse 75, 82–9

Mosley, Alexander 67, 70, 71

Mosley, Charlotte 64–73

Mosley, Diana 68, 70, 71, 73

Mosley, Louis 67

Mosley, Oswald 71

Ney, Michel 97

Nijinsky, Vaslaw 75

Le Nôtre, André 21

Offenbach, Jacques 75

Pagnol, Marcel 121, 155

Palais Royale 101, 128

Parc Montsouris 83

Paris 64–119

Passebon, Pierre 130–7

Pebeyres family 147

Pelissou, Alexis 147

Perriand, Charlotte 132

de Peyrat, Seigneurie 48–55

Picabia 75

Picasso, Pablo 75, 135

Picquier, Dominic 94, 98

Pierre et Gilles 135

Pillet, Christopher 116

Pisanello, Antonio 87

Poincaré, Raymond 68, 71

Provence 8, 12–19, 120–9

Putman, Andrée 8, 109

Quercy 8, 172–9

Quinta, Henri 97, 98

Raffarin, Jean-Pierre 148

Ramier, Suzanne 135

Raphael 87

Rasmussen 136

Rembrandt 178

Richelieu, Armand 101

Rive Gauche 67, 108–19

La Roche 172–9

de Rochechouart, Anne 19

Royau, Jean 136

de Sabanac, Hughes 147, 151

Sacksick, Gilles 8, 164–71

Sacksick, Isabelle 173, 175

Sacré-Coeur 75, 76, 79

Saint Laurent, Yves 126

Saint-Rémy 121–4

Satie, Eric 75

Savahaba, Asha 79

Sempey 169

Le Sentier 100–7

Shakers 188

Sotheby's 55

Stalin, Joseph 83

Starck, Philippe 8, 97, 109

Steinberg, - 81

Stendhal 75

Stefanidis, John 68, 70

studios 82–9

de Suremien, Jean-Baptiste de Flamardin 30, 34

Taulé, Antoni 92, 94, 97

Taulé, Djamila 90–9

La Tour Hughes de Sabanac 146–53

Touraine 130–7

Truffaut, François 75

Tvode, Mogens 66, 67, 73

Uzès, Le Duche d' 7, 12–19

Valadon, Suzanne 116

Valauris 135

Valentino 188

Van Deer, P. 8, 9

Van Gogh, Vincent 121, 122

Vega, Inès 80

Verey, Rosemary 25

Vermeer, Jan 178

La Vie de Bohème 64–119

Viennet, Beatrice 48–55

Viennet, Luc 48–55

Villeroy & Boch 116

da Vinci, Leonardo 131

Warhol, Andy 136

Wyndham, Melissa 54

d'Yvil, Château 33

ACKNOWLEDGEMENTS

First and best thanks must go to the owners of these houses and apartments, for their patience and generous hospitality. I am grateful for special help and advice from Charlotte Mosley, Polly Devlin, Jean Bond Rafferty, Caroline Conran, Patricia Hawkes, Jancis Robinson, Ophélie Renouard, Beatrice Viennet and Ingrid Hudson.

Agents are often described as "long-suffering" and in this case Jane Judd has more than earned the label, and my gratitude. Likewise Lizzy Gray, the painstaking editor at Pavilion. Annaliese Ellidge did invaluable research and additional reporting in Paris, as well as arranging the photoshoots there; we could not have done without her.

Tim Clinch, whose superb pictures bring the homes in the book to life, and I had often collaborated at a distance on articles for *House & Garden*. At the end of this long project we have somehow ended up as neighbours, renovating our own houses in the Languedoc. His humour and energy have been much appreciated – although the sounds of creative demolition from next door can sometimes be alarming. SL